(AND MY
PARSNIP)

GAZ

(AND MY PARSNIP)

GAZ

THE AUTOBIOGRAPHY OF GEORDIE SHORE'S ULTIMATE LAD

JB

JOHN BLAKE

Published by John Blake Publishing Ltd,
3 Bramber Court, 2 Bramber Road,
London W14 9PB, England

www.johnblakepublishing.co.uk

www.facebook.com/johnblakebooks 🔲
twitter.com/jblakebooks 🔲

First published in hardback in 2014
This edition published in 2015

ISBN: 978 1 78418 371 4

British Library Cataloguing-in-Publication Data:

A catalogue record for this book is available from the British Library.

Design by www.envydesign.co.uk

Printed in Great Britain by CPI Group (UK) Ltd

3 5 7 9 10 8 6 4 2

Papers used by John Blake Publishing are natural, recyclable products made
from wood grown in sustainable forests. The manufacturing processes
conform to the environmental regulations of the country of origin.

Every attempt has been made to contact the relevant copyright-holders, but
some were unobtainable. We would be grateful if the appropriate people
could contact us.

CONTENTS

INTRODUCTION

In January 2013 I found myself standing behind a huge curtain, my whole body literally shaking with nerves. I could hear the rumble of thousands of excited people nearby and I knew that all of them had gathered there for one simple reason – to see me.

To make it even more surreal, this was all taking place in a random shopping centre in Australia in the middle of the day – thousands of miles from the UK.

It was something I could never have imagined happening to me: little Gary Beadle from Newcastle.

I've made thousands of promotional appearances since I first appeared on *Geordie Shore* and it never fails to amaze me just how many people want to say hi, shake my hand, or give me a big hug.

Two years on, I'm still trying to figure out how it all came about. I never planned to be on TV and I certainly didn't ever have my heart set on becoming famous. It's been a complete and utter surprise.

But I love my new life and I thank my lucky stars for it when I wake up every single day – usually with a raging hangover!

This is my first book and I've written it for two very specific reasons. Firstly, I wanted people to know the real Gaz – where I came from, who I am and why I do what I do.

Secondly, I wanted to share my pulling tactics and tips, since lots of the people who come up to me for a chat often ask me how I manage to get so many women to come home with me after nights out.

I'm hovering just above the 800 mark at the moment, so I've done pretty well for myself with the lasses over the years. It hasn't all been luck either – I've had to work hard on perfecting my pulling techniques and I hope this book will give you a good insight into all the things I've learned.

There will be some surprises in these pages, I promise you that.

I want to say thank you to my family for supporting me, my friends for sharing this experience with me, and MTV for making it all happen in the first place.

I also need to thank my brilliant management team, Shaq and Kay at IMA, and Tina Campanella, the mint journalist who helped me put this book together.

CHAPTER 1

TOUCH AND GO

I don't shy away from anything. As you'll find out as you read this book, that's how I got on *Geordie Shore* and that's how I've always lived my life – literally from the moment I was born.

I'm also a bit competitive. Okay, okay, I'm proper competitive. I don't like anything or anyone to beat me and I never have. You only have to watch me and my mate Scott going head to head on the show to see that.

But it's this attitude that's got me to where I am today, and I like to think it's probably the only reason I'm even alive. Because when I was born on 22 March 1988, in Hexham, Northumberland, no one could have fancied my chances much.

Apparently I couldn't wait to turn up and start causing trouble, because I was born more than two weeks earlier than I should have been.

I actually spent the first two years of my life in and out of hospital with really bad asthma. And I mean really bad. Bad enough to make me regularly stop breathing.

Mam – her name's Shirley – was a trooper. She already had one kid, my sister Claire, who was two when I came along, plus she had a job in a bank, and now suddenly she had a kid who kept threatening to die on her. It can't have been easy, that's for sure.

The first time I had an asthma attack I was literally a newborn and Mam was terrified. She'd found me all blue and floppy in my cot and called 999 in a panic.

They told her to bring me in, because there was no time for an ambulance and every second mattered if I was going to survive. My tiny airways were closing fast and starving me of oxygen. I can't imagine how scared Mam must have been back then.

My dad, Kevin, drove us to hospital and Mam was on the phone to a doctor the whole time. He kept telling her to keep me conscious, so she repeatedly slapped me in the face, yelling: 'Keep awake!'

But it was no good, and I had lapsed into unconsciousness by the time we arrived at A&E. Quick-thinking doctors stuck me in an oxygen tent, where I would stay for days. No one could tell if it was already too late.

It was touch-and-go for a long time, and the docs told Mam later that if she hadn't found me at the exact moment she did I would have died in my bed. My death would have been attributed to cot death and that would have been the end of me.

I obviously don't remember any of that terrible time, but after I survived that first attack I practically lived in the hospital. Mam says that even then I had an eye for the ladies.

I used to smile at the fittest nurses (I've always had good taste) and they'd tell her I was definitely going to be a heartbreaker when I grew up. Apparently a great big grin works like a charm on the lasses, no matter how old you are.

I was put on loads of steroids to strengthen my lungs and an asthma medication called Ventolin to open my airways, plus I had to wear a nebuliser when I went to sleep. This was a massive piece of kit with a mask attached to it, and I had to wear it all night to keep me breathing. Proper sexy, that's for sure.

But I didn't really know any different, and I was always a happy kid, Mam saw to that. She never showed me how scared she was, she just devoted herself to looking after me and making sure I had an amazing childhood.

My parents split up when I was around three, and I remember very clearly Dad leaving the house on that day. He was a part-time singer in a band and was always out at night performing in clubs and pubs – a bit like me now, I guess – so I don't really remember him being around all the time when I was really little. But that day he packed his bags and walked out and I remember asking, 'Where's Dad going?'

Mam didn't really know what to say, but she made sure that coming from what was termed a 'broken home' back then never affected either me or my sister.

After my parents divorced, they were always friendly and I'd see Dad every Saturday, so we had regular contact. It was great. He'd walk in and sit at the same kitchen table, just as he had when they were married, and Mam would make him a cuppa like she always had. He was never an absent dad or anything. Between us we all made it work and we're still a very close family today.

GAZ (AND MY PARSNIP)

Having asthma didn't stop me being an outdoorsy kid. I grew up on a neat and tidy estate called Ruskin Court, in a small village called Prudhoe, about eight miles outside of Newcastle. I was always out and about doing something. I hated being cooped up indoors.

I used to come tearing down the road on my skateboard or bike and I was always falling over and coming home with cuts and bruises. Mam says now that she could hardly keep up with the things I was doing, because it was always something different. I picked up new skills very easily, especially if there was a ball involved.

Mam always tells this one story: it was a summer's evening and I was outside playing tennis with these two ten-year-old lads. I was hitting the ball all over the place, using nice clean serves, running them ragged, until eventually she came out to fetch me home and to bed. When she got to us, the two older lads were completely out of breath while I was just grinning, tennis racket in hand.

'How old is Gary?' they asked her, wheezing. They were a little embarrassed when she told them I was only three.

At that age I didn't seem to understand that I was really ill and I had no fear at all. I threw myself into everything I did so I must have been a right handful. Although Mam was too nervous at first to take me overseas because of my condition, we always had amazing holidays and days out. We visited water parks and went go-karting and she always made sure we had something fun to look forward to.

When I was old enough to go to school, Mam was still cautious about leaving me alone, so she got a job as a dinner lady there so as to be on the spot in case anything went wrong. Anything could set off my asthma – humid weather, frosty conditions, a cat strolling by – my airways would close and I'd drop to my knees and Mam would have to race me to the hospital. Again.

At my first school, Prudhoe West First School, I loved chasing all the girls in the playground. They'd always tell Mam that they were my girlfriends and I'd innocently pretend I didn't know what she was on about. But I did like having the girls after me, even then.

I may have always been active, but because of the asthma I did have my limits. I noticed that the other kids could keep going for ever while I often struggled to breathe and I didn't like it at all. It was very frustrating.

If I got out of breath I never wanted anyone to know, so I'd hide behind Mam's legs in the playground and ask her to cover for me. It made me determined to beat whatever it was that was stopping me, so I took up every sport there was, in order to get fitter. And I especially liked competitive sport.

Our first proper holiday was to Tenerife where we went when I was about four. Once Mam got a little less scared about me collapsing and dying we holidayed there a couple of times every year without fail.

She bought me this mint T-shirt to wear on my first trip over there – a bit of a warning to everyone, I guess. It read: 'Here comes trouble'...

In the resorts, I'd ask her for spare change and go and challenge the older lads to a game of pool. I didn't really know what I was doing but I figured it out pretty quickly, just so I could beat them. I couldn't even see over the table without standing on a chair, but I'd get the balls down, somehow.

They always held these competitions in the kids' club, where they gave out brightly coloured certificates to the winners. It was like showing a red rag to a bull: I needed to win them – all of them. Whether it was swimming, darts, table tennis… Whatever the contest, I had my eye on winning it.

Mam used to tell me I had to just enjoy taking part, and don't get me wrong, I did, but it was the winning I was most interested in. I just loved being the best.

She taught me how to swim from a very young age and me and my sister were always in swimming galas. Claire used to train all the time and would win the odd bronze and silver medal, while I just turned up to compete and scooped up all the golds through sheer determination.

I may have been good but that didn't mean I didn't occasionally suffer from nerves. I regularly swam for the county but when it got more serious than that I worried I wouldn't win and sometimes that made me bottle it.

And I remember arriving for one important gala and looking at the water and just deciding I wasn't going to get in. Mam tried to convince me, but once my mind is made up I'm like a drunk *Geordie Shore* girl – there's no moving me. I just freaked out and walked away.

It might not seem like it now, but I was actually quite a shy child. I had to really push myself to be the centre of everything, and the easiest way was by winning things, or making everyone laugh.

My grandparents lived nearby and we spent a lot of time with them. My grandad was hilarious, always saying something sarcastic and I saw how happy everyone was when they were laughing. So, following his example, I'd always be cracking jokes or saying stupid things and I did make friends quickly.

At my first school in Prudhoe, the teachers would

probably have described me as a cheeky little chap. I was always the one who would push them that bit too far. I couldn't help myself. Whenever they said something like 'the next kid who laughs gets a detention' – I'd be the one who instantly giggled.

I never had bad reports though. My grades were always high and my homework was always done. It was just that I liked to entertain everyone. At home my family could never get a word in, but that was mainly because they were generally laughing at me.

Mam used to have all the neighbours round on New Year's Eve because she couldn't go out – she had us to look after – and I'd often sneak down to put on a show.

I thought tractors were proper mint when I was a kid, and Mam bought me this little ride-along tractor with a trailer. I'd get on it and show off perfect three-point turns in the lounge until the clock struck midnight.

Our house was the house all the kids gathered in at the weekends. Mam mothered everyone and she didn't bat an eyelid at having 10 or 12 kids in the garden, all racing around. I had football posts set up so that we could kick the ball around for hours.

My best mate on the estate was a lad called Greg Orrock, and we were always getting into scrapes together. We'd go on 'missions', leaving the house first thing and not coming back until it was dark. We'd ride for miles and miles just exploring and building things. We lived in a safe area and I had a lot of freedom really.

We even used to go into the woods near our house and make mini campfires, but that all stopped when one of them got dangerously out of control. Usually they'd only be tiny little fires, and once we'd had our fun we'd put them out with a bottle of water fairly easily. But this one time our flickering flames got too big, too fast and there was nothing we could do to stop it spreading.

We legged it back to my house and watched as the fire engines turned up to sort it out. I remember Mam wondering what all the fuss was about and then trying to guess how it had happened. I never confessed, though I guess I'm confessing to it now. Sorry Mam.

The worst bother I got into was when I was nine. I'd bought a bunch of cheap plastic pellet guns in Tenerife from one of the many market stalls, and when I got back from holiday me and the lads used them to shoot at each other.

It was daft, but all kids are daft when they get together and it was just a bit of harmless fun. We were having a right giggle playing at being Rambo until an old lady who lived nearby came out to see what was going on. Some kid said innocently, 'Oh there's a group of lads with guns and they're firing at us.'

She got straight on the phone and called the police and suddenly the gun squad, the ones in Armed Response Vehicles, was preparing to surround my village.

We didn't know any of this had happened until we heard police sirens getting louder and louder, obviously coming our way. A few cop cars appeared and suddenly a group of coppers were running at us, full pelt. We didn't stop to find out why because we were terrified. We just legged it into the woods. When we got to the other side we stopped and stared: there were 10 police cars on the road ahead of us, forming a blockade, and policemen were everywhere.

They were all wearing bulletproof vests and yelling: 'STOP! Put it down!'

I looked at the gun, which was still in my hand: ah... It all made sense.

'It's plastic!' I yelled back, waving it about a bit for them to see. But they weren't taking any chances.

'Put it down!' they repeated.

So we all did.

As they bundled us all into separate cars we were still protesting that we'd done nothing wrong. They drove me back home and when Mam opened the door she was faced with me, flanked by three CID officers who were all looking very stern.

'It was plastic,' I whined, knowing it wouldn't make a difference – I was still in a heap of trouble.

Mam was horrified. The street was filled with cop cars and everyone was peering out of their windows to see what was going on. Mam quickly explained that I was telling the truth, they were only plastic toys, but she had to go down to the police station and sort it all out.

So I didn't play with guns after that, though Mam wasn't mad at me really. She thought the whole thing had been blown out of proportion, and eventually she saw the funny side.

I generally got away with most things with Mam. I'd just give her a grin and she'd melt. But I was a good kid to her – I always respected my elders and did what I was told. I was just mischievous and hard to keep track of.

If she did give me any punishment, like writing out lines, I'd just get it done without making a fuss. Then I'd come downstairs and give her a smile and say I'd done it and she'd usually let me get on with whatever I'd been doing.

When she grounded me I'd just go and find something to do indoors. I never argued – I generally wanted to keep the peace.

I've always been a lover not a fighter. And I've always been better at hurting myself than other people.

If I wasn't in hospital for my asthma I was there getting stitched back together again after some accident or another.

Like the time I literally got 'Tangoed'.

It was Sports Day at school – the best day of the year as far as I was concerned because I could significantly add to my medal collection. I was barely ten, but I'd collected quite a hoard of winning trophies already.

We were let out early from class to go and sit on the grass of the playing field while everything was being set up and it wasn't long before we were all bored and getting up to no good.

First we started to have a headstand competition to see who could balance for the longest time. But then some bright spark decided to make the challenge a little tougher by throwing bottles of orange Tango at us while we were upside down, to knock us off balance.

'Fair enough, let them take their best shot,' I thought.

Bottles went flying, taking people out left, right and centre but not hurting anyone. And I stayed firmly balanced, even after a few direct hits to the gut.

Soon I was the only one left upside down and was declared the winner. But as I was righting myself to a round of applause, one last bottle of Tango came whizzing through the air and hit me squarely on the back of the head.

Apparently bottles of Tango can split your head open when launched full throttle at you. Who knew that?

There was blood everywhere. The teachers were running around, panicking, and before I knew it both a helicopter and an ambulance had been dispatched to fetch me to hospital.

Head injuries are serious business. But I couldn't believe my luck – a helicopter ride? Bring it on! I thought.

Mam came rushing over just as the helicopter began to circle overhead. It was so loud and everyone was staring at it, gobsmacked. But then I heard another, more familiar sound: the scream of an ambulance siren heading our way.

It had arrived at the same time as the helicopter, so before it could land and pick me up for my ride it was sent to respond to another emergency instead and I had to settle for an ambulance trip.

I was gutted. 'Mam, it was there, it was coming in to land,' I remember saying, as she was freaking out because of all the blood.

We didn't stay long at the hospital, but I had a serious amount of stitches down the back of my head by the time we left. When we got into Mam's car to go home it was only lunchtime, and I was feeling fine. I begged her to take me back to school so I could compete in the sports. She wasn't impressed, but I convinced her in the end. I'd missed out on a helicopter ride, I wasn't going to miss out on Sports Day.

I could still see my blood on the grass when I got back, but I got stuck in right away. To be completely honest, I can't really remember if I won anything, but I'm going to say I did. I deserved to, anyway.

Then there was the time I nearly severed my arm climbing a tree at the back of our estate. I was wearing my favourite Newcastle United strip and playing with the big lads again. We were climbing up and hanging from the biggest branch before dropping to the ground.

It was going well until the lads noticed blood dripping through my shirt from under my arm.

When I lifted it up to take a look all I could see was a great big gash – right through to the bone. I hadn't noticed, but a nylon rope had been hanging from the tree and had passed under my arm as I was falling. The friction had made it slice through my skin like a knife through butter.

So I was whisked off to hospital again, and the doctor told me I'd have to stay the night to have it all stitched back together under a general anaesthetic.

I wasn't impressed. I didn't fancy sleeping in the hospital; I'd done it so many times before and it was very dull. The doctor looked at me for a second and then said that if I was a brave lad, he could do it there under a local anaesthetic instead. That sounded like a much better idea, so I agreed and he got to work.

Surprisingly, I didn't feel a thing as he stitched me back up, but it took a while. The nurses kept me occupied by saying that maybe I'd get a new football strip, if the one I had been wearing was damaged.

I hadn't even thought about it, but it sounded like a good trade for a few stitches. But when Mam lifted up the shirt to take a look no one could believe it: somehow the rope had ripped through my arm and completely missed my shirt, without tearing it at all.

So, no helicopter ride and no new footie shirt: all these injuries and no rewards? I'd be forgiven for feeling a little hard done by.

By the time I was 12, the asthma was finally under control and I was officially discharged from hospital, which was amazing. I'd spent most of my life wearing a nebulizer while sleeping, dealing with not really being able to breathe properly, and although I'd tried not to let it affect me, it had been annoying.

I was in all sorts of football teams and trained for some

sport or another almost every night. So running out of breath or collapsing every now and again was not helpful.

Having grown out of the asthma, I was finally free. It was a good job, too – because I had decided I was going to be a professional footballer when I grew up.

PARSNIP POINTERS

NO. 1: HOLIDAY BANTER

When people go on holiday, it's usually to let off steam and get away from their normal lives for a while. Sex is very good for your health. It releases endorphins and relaxes you. So holiday romances are great for a girl's wellbeing – and even better for your parsnip.

It can be so easy to pull on holiday; all you need is the right banter. The conditions are already ripe for a shag, because everyone is hot and gagging for it. All you need to steer your chosen lass in the direction of your cock is the right arsenal of chat-up lines.

Time is limited when you're on holiday – you can't meet a lass and then take a few days to get to know her. It's all about setting the right scene for a one-night stand, and this is where most lads make their first mistake.

DON'T just steam in and ask if they're up for it. This almost never works, and makes them feel cheap.

DO ease into your banter. Use questions like: 'Where are you from?' 'How long are you here for?' 'How many of you are there?' 'Have you been here before?' 'Where did you go on holiday last year?'

Keep the questions holiday based – don't remind them of back home by asking what they do for a living, for example. You can move onto all of that later, if you run out of conversation. For now, keep her in her hazy holiday world, where the sun is shining, life is good and everyone is free and wants to have a good time. Your job is to convince her that shagging you would make her holiday even better.

These questions should take about 20 minutes, and since you've not yet leaned in for a kiss, it seems like you're actually keen on getting to know her instead of just wanting to get laid.

Hold back. Buy her a drink, dance with her a bit, ask her a few more questions. Then move a little closer and say: 'Fancy a cuddle?'

This makes you seem a lot softer than if you ask for a kiss. Cuddling is so sweet and innocent. But it always leads to something more. Cuddles are a parsnip's first base. They're the first jump on the springboard to sex. From there you can dive right in.

CHAPTER 2

FOOTBALL FANTASIES

When I was at school, if you were good at sports, you were cool. At Prudhoe, I was the captain of the school football team, so I was instantly popular.

I hung around with the other players and a group of cool girls that were part of our crowd. I may have been young but I always had my eye on the fittest girls in the school, and during my time at Prudhoe these were Terri and Hayley. They were both very sporty lasses: Terri was an amazing swimmer and Hayley was a dead fast runner.

Being a cheeky little flirt, I always teased them, but we were all just mates really. We were only nine. I wasn't that bothered about girls at that point because life was all about the football for me.

It was a small school, with only five classrooms, and I liked being popular. I was the fastest runner, the best footballer and life was easy.

I played football in various leagues outside of school too,

because I loved the thrill of the competition. There weren't always sides for me to join but that didn't stop me. I just made up a team and convinced Mam to be our manager. She loved it really.

What's more, I had loads of mates in different areas. They didn't know each other but they all knew me, so I'd convince them to get together and form a team.

Mam would gather us all on a pitch and just tell us to play. Then she'd find leagues for us to join so we could play competitively. We called ourselves the Mickley Magpies, and she ferried us to all our matches in a minibus. Grandad owned a minibus company, which was pretty fortunate.

My mam was such a devoted parent. She was at every training session, every match and she'd do anything to make me happy. She was definitely the only female football manager in our area. I remember that we came runners-up in one league and won another and we loved having the medals hung around our necks. I often won 'Player of the League', and Mam won 'Manager of the League' once too. We were a tidy team, me and Mam.

When I was 10 I moved up to a middle school called Highfield.

It was a much bigger pond than Prudhoe and suddenly I wasn't the biggest fish anymore. There were bigger, taller, older lads everywhere and I confess I was a bit nervous when I first arrived.

I still wore trainers with flashing lights on, which was a bit embarrassing, and I didn't know anyone in my new class. All I heard on that first day was things like 'Jeff is an unreal footballer' or 'Steve's the fastest runner in the school'.

All the fittest girls were talking about lads I didn't know and it made me determined to get a name for myself.

After school that day I heard a group of new girls asking who was on the football team and I knew I'd be okay as long as I got in. It was a guaranteed way into the 'cool crowd', so I couldn't wait for the trials.

Like I've said, although I may not have seemed it, I was still quite shy and being on the football team would mean I didn't really have to introduce myself to everyone – because they would automatically know who I was.

After the tryouts I was made captain and that meant I was sorted. Especially since they had decided I was too good for Year Five and had stuck me in the team for the year above.

From then on, I would be in my lessons and an older lad would knock on the door and say, 'Can Gary come to football now?'

Instant cool.

There were definitely in-crowds and geeky cliques at school but I never got involved with any bullying. I thought it was cruel and generally tried to get along with everyone.

Plus I wasn't just a jock – I didn't let my schoolwork suffer because of sport. I was in all the top sets academically, and I was especially good at maths, so I knew all the brainy kids as well as the sporty ones. I never wanted to be mean to anyone. What would that achieve?

My friend Terri, from Prudhoe, became part of the cool crowd at Highfield too, but I wasn't interested in her as a girlfriend – I now had my sights set on the girl every lad wanted: her name was Gillian and she became the first girl I ever kissed.

Most people my age in Prudhoe hung out on Friday nights

at a swimming pool called Water World. They had a regular event called 'Rave the Wave' where a DJ played music while you splashed around in the water with your mates.

But the locker room was where all the real action went on.

Gillian was a pretty brunette – not sporty like the kind of girl I usually got on with, but then again I'd never really wanted to kiss those girls: they were just mates. Gillian was different. She was girly and sweet and always looked perfect. Everyone wanted her, so I naturally did too. But I would never have approached her.

So it was lucky that when I was 13 that someone came up to me in Water World and announced: 'Gillian wants to kiss you by the lockers.'

I couldn't believe she'd chosen me and as the words sunk in I was, quite frankly, shitting myself. I didn't know whether you used tongues or whatever when you kissed. My mates had all done it but we'd never discussed the finer details – it was just something everyone did.

I pretended it was completely normal and that I totally knew what I was doing. I went to meet her and we locked lips for a bit. It was literally just fish kissing, but when it was over I strutted back out to the pool feeling like a fucking king.

It obviously hadn't been that bad for her either, because she gave me her house number and said I could go round some time. And I did. Often.

I'd get on my BMX and ride round to her house and we'd just sit and kiss on her bed. It was good practice.

Over the next few years, my life revolved around football and girls. I'd hang round at one of the lads' houses, or just out on the street with everyone, and we'd meet up with the girls and just snog our way through them. We never really did anything more than that. It was all quite innocent really. Not like nowadays where kids start shagging at a really young age.

I'll probably get blamed for that because of *Geordie Shore*, but I don't agree with it. Best to keep it in your pants till you're older, kids...

Even back then, I was very discerning about who I kissed. I only picked the coolest girls. But even so, I must have got through about 30 before I turned 15. Like everything in my life I saw it as a competition, and I wanted to kiss the most girls out of everyone.

In football, I was also racing ahead. Our school 11-a-side team was brilliant, and we won the school league the first year I was there. Our head teacher, Mr Sample, took us all out for McDonald's to celebrate and I remember thinking that was amazing. Buying everyone McDonald's? What a legend.

Out of the best players in that 11-a-side team, our coach Mr Stanton picked the six best players to play in a national six-a-side tournament. I was one of the special six.

It was a big deal. The final was being held at Wembley and I couldn't even begin to imagine how exciting it would be to play there – the home of British football.

We beat 10 other schools in the North East to win the regional round. Then we beat everyone else in the north of England and made it through to the semi-finals.

By that time, we were literally famous. All the local news-papers wrote about us and everyone at school knew who I was. We only had one more team to beat before we could plan our Wembley takeover. But we were knocked out in our semi-final match, and our Wembley dreams instantly died a pretty painful death.

To get that far and not make it was absolutely devastating.

Mam was there, Grandad was there – they were both gutted too. All the lads on my team were actually crying as we walked off the pitch. It was one of the biggest disappointments of my life. But Mam said there would always be more tournaments, and she was right.

I was still playing in leagues outside of school, and I'd moved up from our local team in Prudhoe to play for a better team called Stocksfield FC, which was in the Northern Football Alliance.

It meant that outside of school I played against most of my schoolmates rather than alongside them, and we always beat them. It was a posh team, which always made me laugh. One of the lads' dads was the best barrister in the country. It was practically high society.

We had this wicked goalie, the best I'd ever seen. His name was Fraser Foster and he became a good mate of mine.

After the six-a-side tournament which finished at Wembley, I was scouted by an even better team called Grainger Park, which was based in Newcastle.

In Newcastle, all the top players, like Alan Shearer, came up from playing in a team called the Wallsend Boys Club. Grainger Park was in the same league as that team, so if you played well you could definitely get noticed by the right people.

While I settled in I heard talk that they were looking for a goalie too, and I remembered Fraser and recommended him. He was a shy kid, quiet, but a nice lad. He came for trials and they wanted him immediately. He really was an amazing goalie.

In our first season at Grainger Park the manager there got a scout from Scotland to come and see him. From that point on, everyone went nuts for Fraser. He was eventually signed by Newcastle FC, then Norwich, before Celtic FC signed him off them – and he's still at Celtic today.

We couldn't believe it when he went to play for Newcastle. I was proud of the lad, especially since it was me who got him into Grainger Park.

Everyone was convinced I was going to follow in his footsteps and play for Newcastle. It was my dream. At school, when everyone chatted about the future, everyone was pretty matter-of-fact about mine. 'Gaz? Oh, he's going to play for the Toon,' they'd say.

There literally wasn't anything else I could imagine doing.

I trained most evenings and weekends, and I knew I was good. I just needed to get scouted and that took both time and luck.

When I was 12, Grainger Park made it through to a European league, and we all flew to Barcelona for the tournament. It was amazing. Mam and Claire flew out with us, and she was one of only three mams there. Everyone else had their dads with them, but Mam was the one who had supported me throughout my footie career, so she was buzzing to come along. Claire wasn't quite so keen on football but Mam brought her anyway. Mam has always liked to keep the family tight – she's still the linchpin holding everything together for us all. She's got very strong values and, despite how it sometimes looks, they have rubbed off on me.

She believes family is everything, and you have to stick by them through thick and thin. Even now, in the *Geordie Shore* house, we're all like one big family and that's why I can't take it when we all fight. It goes against everything I was taught by Mam and I hate it.

GAZ (AND MY PARSNIP)

The whole Grainger Park team went on the tour to Barcelona, and our coach halved the 15-strong squad into an A team and a B team, because it was a 7-a-side tournament.

I was in the B team, which I wasn't happy about. Mam said it was because the coach and the trainer had sons in the squad, and they'd got their dads to put all their best mates in the A team alongside them. It seemed unfair, but it just made me determined to wipe the floor with the lot of them.

The whole tournament was an amazing experience. The other European teams all had full matching kit and tracksuits, right down to their socks, and would go into the stadium changing blocks to get changed into their pristine outfits before their matches.

We'd just stick on our plain kit in the hotel and turn up to face all these neatly turned out players and smash them. It was very satisfying.

Mam watched all the games alongside the managers and trainers. She deserved to – she'd been so involved in everything I did at the club.

In the semi-finals, we actually faced our A team and we definitely felt like we had something to prove. It was a tough match. At half-time it was nil-nil and at full-time it was 1-1, so it went to extra time and then penalties.

Eventually, we beat them.

The A team were crying their eyes out and I began laughing at them all. 'That'll teach them for all that favouritism,' I thought. But I stopped when Mam gave me one of her stern looks.

In the final, we faced Italy. As we set about giving their team a proper thrashing I couldn't believe we'd come so far.

It felt like a proper professional tournament and I hoped it was a sign of things to come. Especially when we won 3-1. I scored one of the goals and ran round the pitch like a nutter, screaming and cheering.

At the end of the tournament, all the teams attended the presentation ceremony, which was like something out of a movie. Standing in line with my team, I could see two trophies on the table, and couldn't wait to lift one of them up.

So when the second and third placed teams came up and were handed them, one after another, I was a bit confused. The table was now empty. Where was our trophy?

By this time, it had started to get dark. Suddenly, 'We are the Champions' began playing through the stadium speakers and all these fireworks began going off all around us. Then this guy in a cape came down on a wire and handed us this gigantic trophy. We were all a bit shocked as we gratefully took it off him. Mam said it was like winning the World Cup and it definitely felt like it to us lads.

When I got back home, I began playing for the county. My school coach had put me and this other guy called Jeff Maskell forward for the county team and when I got in Mam was buzzing. It was a huge step up and I felt like I was really on my way.

I was putting in the hours training, and I didn't drink or smoke like many other lads my age. I didn't even like it if Mam had a drink, which was a rare event in itself. I'd tell her off if I saw her with even a shandy.

Back then I was dead against alcohol, which obviously seems funny now, with the amount I can put away. But looking back on it I think it was because I wanted to be in control of my own life. After so many years not really having any control over my own body because of the asthma, I wanted to feel like I was finally in charge of it. And I couldn't be in charge of it if I got drunk, because I knew that alcohol made you lose control.

I'd seen people slurring their words and falling over after having a skinful, and I couldn't understand why anyone would choose to let that happen.

It also kind of explains why I was so competitive as a kid: if I couldn't beat something that was taking away the very air that I breathed, then I would try and beat everything else to prove I was in control.

I wanted to be in charge of my own destiny, and entering my teenage years I was convinced that my destiny was to be a professional footballer. And I wouldn't let anything stand in my way, so drinking and smoking were definitely out.

Even now, I never get so loaded that I don't know what I'm doing. I get drunk, I could never deny that, but I don't get to the point where I'm not in control.

I do the things I do because I want to – not because I'm told to, or because I think I have to. I drink now because I like it. I have sex a lot because I enjoy it. And I played football because I loved nothing better than tearing through a team's defence and putting one away in the back of the net.

I believed I was good enough to go pro and that it was my destiny to make it happen. So when I got home from school one day near the end of the school year to find Mam waving an important envelope around in a state of near madness, I knew it could mean only one thing.

The letter was addressed to me, and it had the Newcastle FC logo on it. 'It's from The Club,' Mam said, shaking with excitement.

I opened it up and read the words I'd hoped for for years:

FOOTBALL FANTASIES

We'd like you to come to trials at Newcastle Football Club...

It was every lad's dream and I was finally living it.

I didn't have much time to prepare – the trials would last six weeks and would take place in the school summer holidays at the club's training grounds: *the club's real training grounds!*

I read out loud that training would take place a few times a week and we'd have a match every Saturday. Mam instantly began crying. Bless her – she wanted it as much as I did.

For some reason, I turned up for the first training session wearing a Barcelona shirt. I looked around at everyone else in black and white stripes and thought, 'shit'.

But I soon got over it, and I worked so hard that summer.

While all my mates were chilling with each other in the sunshine, I was doing sprints and learning greater ball control and doing my absolute best to stand out from the crowd.

For our first match, which was against Sunderland, I walked into the changing rooms to see the Newcastle kit hung up on my own peg, ready for me to wear.

It was one of those moments you never forget. My heroes at the time were Shearer, Ferdinand, Ginola – they all got to wear this hallowed strip. Now it was my turn. But it wasn't without its issues.

They kept playing me right wing, which I couldn't understand as I was a striker – a glory hunter. I only got to play in my rightful position once, and I did score, but I wasn't a defender and I guess that's what they were seeing the whole time I was there.

At the end of the trials I went home and waited to hear whether I'd made it into the youth team. But when I tore open the letter I finally received, it didn't read like I wanted it to.

I hadn't made it.

I was gutted.

It was my first experience of failure and I didn't know how to take it. I'd always been the best, and now I had proof that I wasn't. It was a hard lesson to learn.

Plus, I didn't have a clue what I was going to do with my life instead. I could still play football, for Grainger Park and the county, and I was good, I knew that. But obviously I wasn't the best.

So, if I wasn't going to be a professional footballer, what would I be? It was a question I would struggle with for many years.

PARSNIP POINTERS

NO. 2: POOL PULLING

Holidays are like pulling playgrounds. Everyone is hot and wearing very little, drinking loads and wanting to let off steam. And the easiest way to bag a bird is to get her in the pool.

Pools are good for a number of reasons. Girls don't really sunbathe with their full warpaint on, so you can see whether they're really fit right away, without being tricked by low lighting and layers of fake eyelashes.

If she looks hot with no make-up, she's going to look insane at night, all done up. If a girl is a seven or an eight just lying by the pool, she's going to be a solid 10 at night. Remember that.

So you spot a girl, she's basking in the sun, the best thing to do is start up a conversation, using the holiday pulling lines I've already suggested.

Take it easy, this is just a relaxing chat, so don't get too heavy. When you're ready, sigh deeply and remark how hot it is. Then simply ask if they fancy a dip. No girl is going to say no – it's always hot abroad and it feels good to cool down.

Once you get her in, lead her like a little lamb to the deep end – you'll probably be taller than her, so offer her a hand. As it gets too deep, pull her gently towards you.

She has to grab hold of you to keep afloat, and bingo, you are now skin to skin, and it's taken you mere seconds. This would never happen that quickly in a club.

Pools are not just for swimming…

Now that you're touching, it's time to flirt a little more strongly. You're touching, you're half naked, it's hot and steamy… It's only a matter of time before you kiss.

Time it right, and it's job done.

CHAPTER 3

FIRST LOVE

When I was 13 I left Highfield and went to Prudhoe High School. My sister was already a student there, and one of my neighbours, James Ostell, was set to start there too. So although I should have been nervous starting another school, I wasn't at all.

James and I were really excited. After years of hanging around with each other we could actually walk to school together too. When we arrived, I introduced him to the kids I knew and he did the same. And so, by the time I tried out for the school footie team, I pretty much knew everyone. Especially since I'd played against most of them outside of school too.

This time I shared the captaincy with a lad called Jeff.

I asked some of the lads who the fittest girls in the year were, and I was given four or five names. They were all pretty girls, but there was one I fell for, hook, line and sinker, and her name was Laura.

GAZ (AND MY PARSNIP)

It didn't take me long to start kissing a stream of girls from my year, but Laura was special. I actually thought I could date her. You know – be her boyfriend. It was the first time I'd even considered having a relationship with someone.

I tried to catch her eye and got a mate to tell her I liked her. We started to become friends and chatted on MSN messenger – we didn't have mobile phones way back then – but before I could seal the deal she was snapped up by someone else.

There were two lads a few years above me who pretty much ruled the school. Jonny Barrett and Nicky Kerr. It was Jonny who swooped in and took Laura away from me, and for more than a year those two were rock solid.

We were still mates and we always got on, but I would stare at her from afar, longingly – I couldn't have her. Yet. It only made me want her more.

Jonny's mate Nicky was the captain of his year, the hardest boy in the school and the best looking lad by far. Everyone loved him. He was a bit of a Jack the Lad – cocky but irresistible. He'd pull a girl, get rid of her the next day and she still wouldn't have a bad word to say about him.

I'd sit and wonder – how does he do it?

Life began to change during those years, as it does for everyone. I began to feel more like an adult than a child, and stayed out later and later with my mates.

We hung around at the local community centre, or in the park, and had house parties whenever anyone's parents were away. Nicky would often be there and I watched him work his magic closely, trying to figure out what made him so special.

Everyone just wanted to get drunk all the time and at this point I still wasn't keen on booze. So while everyone was necking cans of lager I was concentrating on the girls. And believe me, they liked the attention.

One of the girls I used to fumble around with quite a lot was called Harriet, a brunette with long hair and amazing eyes. I prefer blondes, but for some reason I usually end up with smoking-hot brunettes. What a chore.

Harriet and I would often kiss when we were out with our mates, or at school, but then one day she asked me to go round to her house after school and I had a feeling things might go a bit further than normal.

I was only 15, but that wasn't going to stop me if it came down to it. I definitely made sure I had a condom before I went.

So I raced home from school, changed out of my uniform and spruced myself up a bit. Then I left my house and made my way over to her place in the early evening.

On the way to her house, I started to get nervous. I'd never had sex before, or even really got anywhere near that far with a lass. Sex. It was all anyone ever really talked about in our early teens. The few guys who had 'done it' gloated about it with satisfaction, and the lads who hadn't would listen in awe, wondering when it would finally be their turn.

We weren't unique. Mine is a schooldays story that almost every adult will recall. Most people will admit their first time wasn't earth shattering. But it's almost always ground-breaking. I guess that is why as kids we are told to wait as long as possible before losing our virginity. It's the moment we feel that we turn into an adult. And if we're not old enough to see it like that, and feel a bit nervous about it, we probably shouldn't be having sex.

GAZ (AND MY PARSNIP)

I was nervous. I knew that having sex was a big moment in my life and I felt I was ready.

Harriet had done it before, which made it even more nerve-wracking. I was a novice; to me she was an 'experienced woman', although she'd probably only had sex once or twice. She was a nice girl, not the town bike or anything.

And on top of all that, as I walked the five miles between my house and hers, I wasn't even sure whether it would take place. It was only a feeling I had. I knew I had to play it cool and let whatever was going to happen, happen by itself.

Her parents were at home when I arrived, so when I went up to her room we put some music on for background noise before we started kissing.

She had pink fairy lights which lit the room just enough, without it being too dark or too light. I remember thinking that it was actually a pretty perfect setting for a first time, if that was what this was going to be.

When she finally moved me over to her bed all I could think was, 'Oh fuck...' It was really going to happen.

She took control of things, and I was happy to let her take the lead. I lay on the bed, just in awe of what we were about to do together. She climbed on top and began to jiggle away.

Thirty seconds later it was so good I couldn't help it: I came.

I was too scared to tell her so I just let her keep going. But I could feel my dick going soft and I knew it would only be a matter of time before she noticed.

I left it as long as possible, but eventually I had to tell her. Honesty is the best policy and all that... We lay on the bed for a little while longer, before I told her I had a long walk home so I had to get going.

But I didn't walk: I strutted.

It was a huge weight off my shoulders. Not because of peer pressure or anything – I didn't do it to be popular. But I was no longer a virgin and it was a huge step towards being an adult.

It wasn't like everyone was doing it. Most people were just snogging, there weren't that many people in our year shagging. Now it seems like everyone is 14 and having sex like it's no big deal. Maybe it is our fault. Maybe they watch *Geordie Shore* and think it's cool. But we're adults. And it's a TV show. I don't think it's cool to have sex when you're essentially still a child.

You've got to have respect for it. I do believe that, whatever it may seem. And for your partner.

The next morning I met James as usual to walk to school.

'I had it last night,' I told him, proudly.

Everyone knew by the time we got to Prudhoe High. The gossip network among teenagers is prolific, even without mobile phones. I'll admit I felt a bit like a rock star that day.

I didn't go on to date Harriet, we just stayed friends. But I did start to have sex as often as I could.

I was still going on my regular family holidays to Tenerife and I met a lot of girls that way. The sun, the sea, the pool – I very quickly figured out that it all made for easy pickings. After all, the girls are already half naked before you start chatting them up. A bit of splashing around and it's easy to take things a little further. I loved it.

At home I spent my time going to house parties and pulling girls. But I was still getting good grades. In maths, I was the first person in our year to figure out the formula for our GCSE coursework, and I would eventually get an A* in business studies. I was also good at history, even if I did have a bit of help from a less-than-credible historical resource...

GAZ (AND MY PARSNIP)

We had to do a War Diary one term, and I'd been playing the video game *Max Payne* for ages. I loved all the quotes 'Max' used onscreen and they fitted pretty perfectly into what I had to write, so I started to use them. A lot.

When I handed it in my teacher was stunned. She said: 'This is insane!'

I tried to look innocent. 'Is it alright?' I asked.

'It's A-level pass standard,' she told me, and then read it out to everyone. Who knew Max Payne was a literary genius?

Obviously I never owned up to my blatant plagiarism. If I was clever enough to use a unique source, I felt I deserved the credit.

Because I was good at football, I soon began to get invited to the sixth form parties, which were a whole new ballgame from the small gatherings I was used to.

One night, I heard that a girl called Christy was having a party and I'd been invited to go along. Christy was hot. She didn't have to wear school uniform because she was in the sixth form, and she always wore these skintight jeans that made everyone stare at her amazing arse.

Her parties were pretty legendary, and when I got there I immediately spotted Nicky Kerr and his group having a few drinks. I obviously knew Nicky, but had never really talked to him properly.

Like I said before, his lads were the ones who got all the girls. They were the school legends, and nobody messed with them.

After a while he caught my eye and motioned for me to come over.

'Hey lad, how's it going?' he said, and we got chatting.

I must have made him laugh or something, because he seemed to like me. So I stuck around.

'How many girls have you had then, Gaz?' he eventually asked as the conversation turned more personal.

I shrugged. 'About 10 I reckon. You?'

He seemed surprised. 'Twenty-three,' he said.

He was only 17. Like I said, he was the man.

'I'm gonna take you under my wing,' he said decisively, and laughed. 'You can be my young apprentice.'

I didn't argue. Nicky had some kind of magic power with women and I wanted to have it too.

'Alright,' I agreed. 'But I'm gonna catch you up, you wait and see.'

He burst out laughing, as if to say *whatever*. I was such a cheeky little git I got away with everything. From then on Nicky became one of my best mates.

I played footie with him and his friends, and went out on nights with them – he'd come and knock on my door and take me to where all the Year 11 fit girls hung out. So I started pulling all the older birds because I had an in with them through Nicky.

He was as good as his word about teaching me everything he knew. Nicky's special power was that he treated all girls with respect, and I learnt off him pretty quickly that you always have to be honest about your intentions and leave the lasses still liking you when you move on.

If they liked you, and told their mates that you were nice, you'd immediately have a chance with them too, once enough time had passed. Girls gossip. It's a powerful pulling weapon! If you are a shit to them and they tell their mates that, you have no chance with any of them. They close ranks and you're out.

It was quite simple, but very effective.

Then I got to know all his mates, like Jonny, who was still dating my Laura, and a lad called Richie, and it gave me a lot of kudos. It was also like having a couple of older brothers at school and people learnt pretty quickly not to mess with me.

I hated fighting, but if someone started on me, Nicky and Richie would be there in seconds. Nicky told me: 'If anyone touches you, tell them Richie will be seeing them.'

It worked. I was golden.

We were all competitive about pulling girls and my numbers quickly stacked up. But Nicky was always one step ahead of me. Then Laura split up with Jonny and my priorities changed.

I'd wanted her for two years. No girl I'd shagged could compare with her. She was funny and sweet and very, very fit. I'd never been able to have her, which made her all the more appealing.

I obviously couldn't start going after her right away, because Jonny was my mate. But it was obvious that Laura liked me too and eventually he was the one that told me to go for it.

We were already close friends, so it didn't take much for us to become an item. She was my first girlfriend and we were inseparable from the moment we got together.

I quickly fell in love – that kind of puppy love that you never get again. I adored her. I spent most nights at her house, getting to know her parents and the rest of her family. Suddenly I wasn't going out and hanging around trying to pull girls, I was at Laura's watching a movie, or going for weekends to London with her.

We made a memory book of our first time there together, which I've still got. It's filled with tickets from things we went to see, like the musical *We Will Rock You*, and little notes on everything we did.

Laura and I went to the school prom together – me wearing a tux and her wearing a stunning red dress. We even went on holiday to Spain together.

As much as losing my virginity had been a landmark, having my first proper girlfriend was another step on the road to adulthood. I felt more grown up than I ever had before. As one half of a cool couple, my life was good.

I turned 16 and got myself a scooter. Then I got my first job and began to save up for my first car. Suddenly I was washing dishes three times a week in a local Italian restaurant while studying for my GCSEs and seriously beginning to wonder what on earth I would do with my life.

By then I had stopped playing football competitively and only really played in pub leagues for fun. I'd accepted I wasn't going to be a professional player, but I still hadn't decided what I was going to do instead. It was a strange time.

I felt like an adult, doing adult relationship things with Laura, but at the same time I was at school and had no real direction.

And I was still a bit of a handful at home.

That Halloween, me and James Ostell decided with two other lads to egg windows for a laugh. We ran through our estate, hurling them at our unsuspecting neighbours' houses and taking off before anyone could see it was us.

Unfortunately, one guy looked out of his window at the exact moment an egg exploded on the glass pane in front of him.

Me and James looked at each other.

Then we looked back at the guy.

He'd definitely seen our faces.

When he began to leg it towards his front door to confront us, we all scarpered, running as fast as we could down through the back lanes to the main road. We were still panting and laughing when the guy pulled up next to us in his van, looking more than a bit mad.

We all legged it again but he managed to catch James and slung him in the back of his van to interrogate him. I had no idea what had happened and kept running for a long time until I was at a safe distance away and tried to figure out what to do next. Then my phone rang, and I could see it was Mam.

I tried to put on a calm voice as I answered.

'How's your night going?' she asked.

'Oh, it's alright, I'm just out with James,' I lied. I had no idea where James was now. But unfortunately Mam did.

'Hardly,' she said angrily. 'Because James is here with a very angry man at the door. Get home. Now.'

Busted.

When I got back, James and I sat on the sofa, sheepishly, as the guy ranted at Mam. Then he called the police, who turned up and gave us a bit of a talking to. Mam wasn't impressed. At all.

But we were still kids really, doing daft kid things. Half-child, half-adult. As I said, it was a tricky time. It is for all teens.

At that point, we were all preparing to take our GCSE exams. Everyone was deciding whether to do A-levels, and I just didn't have a clue. I wasn't sure I wanted to, but then what else could I do?

NO. 3: SEALING THE DEAL

So you've been chatting up a girl and it's going well, but her annoying friend is hanging around stopping you from taking things further. You think you're going to be screwed, and not in the right way? Think again. You CAN get her alone without looking like a dickhead.

I used to ignore the mate and concentrate only on the girl I wanted to pull, hoping they'd take the hint and leave. But it generally ended badly.

At the end of the night it almost always got to the point where the lass would tell her mate she was going home with me and the mate usually kicked off, causing a scene.

Drama does not lead to sex. It usually leads to a brush-off. After all that work, you've just been wasting your time.

But you can pull a girl when she's out with a mate. It just takes a little time and patience. Here's what you do...

So you've zeroed in on a girl and you can see she's interested. Good work. Now take some time to involve the friend. Ask her about herself, buy them both drinks, take the two of them onto the dance floor.

You're all having fun, she's giving you the eye, but her friend doesn't mind because she trusts you. You're not leaving her out, so you can't only be interested in one thing.

Her mate is starting to trust you, so at the end of the night when the girl you're after tells her she's going home with you, she approves.

You're a nice lad – she knows that because you've been

sweet to them both all night. Soon enough you'll be safely enjoying some well-earned bedroom gymnastics, having successfully got your bird away from her clingy mate.

CHAPTER 4

IN THE NAVY

I had some big decisions to make, but at least I wasn't alone. Everyone I knew was trying to figure out what kind of career they eventually wanted to have and my mates were all struggling as much as I was to decide.

There was one friend, Scott Johnson, who like me wasn't keen on the thought of higher education. His dad took us out one day to try and get us away from the pressures of revision and we ended up in Newcastle, where a massive Navy ship was temporarily docked.

It was huge – an awesome beast of a ship – and we got chatting to a recruiter about what it was like to be a Royal Marine.

I'd always been a big fan of combat games and war films, which I'd watched with my grandad all my life. But I'd never really thought about joining any of the armed forces before, because I'd never really liked the idea of fighting.

Listening to what this guy was saying I began to change my

mind. It wasn't all about fighting, he said, there were plenty of different roles that were important other than the front-line forces. It was mainly about being in peak physical condition, and ready for any challenge.

He told us the running times and fitness levels needed for entry, and explained how tough the physical requirements were.

It sounded like a huge challenge, but one I would be well suited for. I was on the school cross-country team and regularly beat boys much older than myself in time trials. The times he was spouting out were impressive, but I had no doubt I could smash them. He revealed that the Navy even had its own football team, which went on tour. It sounded amazing. Then he said sternly: 'To be in the Royal Marines you have to be the best of the best.'

Although I didn't know it then, I think it was those words that eventually convinced me to sign up. I wanted to be the best of the best. I always had. Maybe this was my path to glory...

My mate Scott felt the same way. As we walked away, I said to him: 'We could do that, you know.'

I began to look into it as an option, and the more I researched, the more it seemed like being a marine would open up a whole world of new job possibilities. I could be in communications, or engineering. I could be a physical trainer, or a sniper.

It would mean I didn't have decide on my career yet – I would be in training for a long time, which was mostly physical work, and at least it was a job that would keep me fit and active. The money was good and I would get to travel: it really did sound perfect for me.

I spoke to Mam and we discussed my options. I was just about to take my GCSEs, and so I could either stay on and do A-levels and then go on to university, leave school and get an office job somewhere, or join the marines.

It was a no-brainer. The marines it was.

Me and Scott began training hard in preparation for enlisting. It would be hard to even get in, so we knew we had to get ready for some stiff competition. *The best of the best*: it certainly wouldn't be easy.

We filled our rucksacks with sand and went on 10-mile runs together. I began doing endless sit-ups and press-ups before I went to bed, and got fitter than I had ever been in my life.

At school, our PE teacher, Mr Rogers, stayed after classes to give us bleep tests and teach us how to climb up ropes and do other things we'd have to do to get in. He was so supportive, and it all felt really exciting.

Soon everyone at school had heard of our plans and were in awe of us. The girls would watch us as we trained, and we got a lot of attention, although I was still going out with Laura, so I mostly ignored their admiring glances.

I took my GCSEs and did well. All my grades were A* to C, apart from French. I hated French and I got an F. I was no cunning linguist back then...

When we felt we were ready, Scott and I formally applied to be Royal Marines and began the long process of enlisting.

The first thing we had to do was take the Royal Marines pre-joining Fitness Test, which involved two timed tread-mill runs of 1.5 miles, with the treadmill set at a 2 per cent incline.

To pass, we had to do the first run in under 12 minutes

and 30 seconds. Then we had to complete the second run, immediately afterwards, in less than 10 minutes.

That seemed straightforward. Scott and I were both very fit, and I'd been running cross-country for years. We both passed and were invited to attend the two-day Potential Royal Marines Course in Lympstone, Devon, at the famous Commando Training Centre.

It was the beginning of the summer. If we passed, we would be given a start date that was approximately three months away – so while everyone else started sixth form, we'd be off doing basic training. It almost didn't feel real.

But when we got off the train in Devon and found ourselves with 90 other applicants settling into the basic army barracks on the first evening, it suddenly felt very real indeed.

We were briefed on what we would be expected to do in the days ahead, and then issued with the appropriate clothing and boots.

We toured the facilities and chatted with some of the other applicants. Everyone was fit and determined. Some of the lads even went to bed early to read Royal Marine biographies, in preparation for the interview part of the trial.

I was nowhere near that prepared. But I didn't like to fail, and that would be my biggest weapon in the two days ahead.

The next day we were up early and marched to a huge computer room, where we all sat a written test to check our maths and English abilities.

Then we were taken outside and sent off on a three-mile run. The first half was done as a group, and the second was practically a solo sprint. It was a giant competition, against lads who were all as fit, if not fitter, than me. I loved trying to beat them all. I was in my element.

Once that was done, it was time to get in the gym for the infamous bleep test. For those who never had to do it at school, it's basically a run back and forth between two lines, set at 20 metres apart, at a pace dictated by a series of beeps.

Each level has several 'shuttle runs' at the same pace, and as the levels go up, the pace quickens. It gets tiring very quickly. Our target was to reach level 13, where the beeps were just over 4 seconds apart.

By this time we'd have run back and forth 131 times, covering a distance of 2,620 metres in just over 13 minutes.

If you didn't make it to the line within the beep at any point during the test you were out. Guys were dropping like flies all around us, but me and Scott made it to the final beep, panting like crazy. It was very, very tough.

After that we had to complete as many sit-ups as possible in two minutes, followed by as many press-ups as we could do in the same time. We had to do 60 press-ups and 80 sit-ups for maximum points.

I managed it and felt like I was flying through the course.

Finally we had to perform 8 full pull-ups on an overhead beam, and climb a rope to the ceiling using just our arms before our physical work was done for the day.

Yet again I was on target.

After a quick shower and change, we all then had a long interview with our course corporal, where we were drilled on our understanding of the Corps and had to prove we were serious about a career in the Royal Marines. I couldn't get away with using Max Payne quotes in there, that's for sure, but I was enthusiastic and made sure I came across as keen.

That night, we were all exhausted, but I was buzzing and so was Scott. Everything about it so far had been amazing. We were pushing ourselves, competing against one another, and focusing as hard as we could at really being the best we could be. It felt empowering.

The next day they didn't take it easy on us. They took us back outside and we had to run around while carrying someone else on our backs. We had to do sprints, press-ups, piggyback rides – it was relentless. And then, just when we were totally knackered, we were told to do the infamous Marine Assault Course.

We set off in groups of three, and I did love it, despite being exhausted from the intense workout they'd already given us. Climbing up ropes, jumping over logs, crawling through the grass – it was a difficult course, but I beat the other two lads in my group to the finish line.

Out of the 90 people who had travelled down to Lympstone, only 13 passed the two-day test.

Scott was one, and I was another.

I was saluted and told I was going to be a Royal Marine. Finally my life had direction again.

We travelled back to Prudhoe and I told Mam that I'd made it in. She was proud of us, I could see that, but I could also see she was really scared. Who wouldn't be? Her 16-year-old son was moving away from home to learn how to be one of the toughest men in the world. There were no guarantees in life – I could die crossing the road the next day – but I would quite possibly soon be putting myself in the way of extreme danger, which significantly upped the chances of my early demise.

I was given my start date, which was 19 October.

That meant I had three months to prepare myself and say

goodbye to all my friends – including Laura. I had a good life, a good set of friends, a beautiful girlfriend: it felt strange to be leaving it all.

Laura tried to be brave. She promised me she'd stick by me and told me she loved me. But we pretty much tried to put it out of our minds for the summer so that we could enjoy our last few months together.

And I focused on my fitness to prepare for the 32-week basic training that I was about to go through. It is widely perceived as the toughest and longest basic training programme in the world, and I knew I'd need to be as ready as possible for it.

I spent as much time as I could with my mates and with Laura and everyone was excited for me. I spent the summer bombing around on my scooter between my house and Laura's, and hanging out with Nicky and the lads.

When September arrived, all my mates went back to school to start sixth form and I was left at home, alone with my thoughts. It began to feel very real and very serious. I was joining the Navy.

But with everyone busy at school, I also got bored. Nicky had left school but he was working on a building site so he wasn't around either. There was only so much training I could do in a day, and other than that I was just waiting for my start date to arrive.

Sometimes the minutes felt like hours. And sometimes I felt a bit mischievous...

My sister had recently passed her driving test and got her first car. I was desperate to start driving, and had a year to go before I could even start taking lessons. But it all looked pretty easy, and I'd always been good on my mini tractor, so I was convinced I could do it.

GAZ (AND MY PARSNIP)

I know it sounds silly, but I was really good on that tractor as a kid. As a toddler I'd got the hang of three-point turns, reversing round corners, and I felt I could handle a motor pretty well.

Besides: I was the best of the best, wasn't I?

I had no doubt I could drive.

On one of those slow, dull days in September everyone was out and the estate was suffocatingly quiet. Claire's car was just sat on the driveway, challenging me to take it for a spin. Every time I looked out of my window, the car was there, saying: *get in, you know you want to...*

I knew where Claire's keys were. So I picked them up and at first just sat in the car with the engine running. But it wasn't long before I was backing out of the drive and making my way down our road to Prudhoe town centre.

Driving was easy. There was nothing to it. I was quite happily cruising along and no one could tell I didn't have a licence. I went over to my old school and caught up with some of my mates. It was great, and so far I had got away with my little turn at *Grand Theft Auto*.

The problem was, I could hardly see over the wheel. I wasn't very tall, and so when a policewoman saw this little lad craning his neck to see through the windscreen, she got a bit suspicious and began following me as I made my way home.

When she eventually pulled me over I decided to try and talk my way out of the situation. As if that was going to work.

Sadly, for all my maths prowess, I gave her the wrong year for my supposed age when she asked for my date of birth and it was then that I knew I was well and truly busted.

Even if I had got it right I doubt I'd have got away with it – she would have next asked to see my licence and I didn't even have a provisional one!

Of course I continued to try to blag my way out of it, saying I didn't have the right documents with me, and she told me I had a day to produce my licence at the local police station or I'd be arrested.

I thanked her and drove home, wondering how on earth I was going to get myself out of this mess – I was about to join the marines, I couldn't get slung in jail before I'd even begun training.

Since I was a good driver, there wasn't a scratch on Claire's car. I pointed this out to Mam when she got home but it didn't soften the telling off I got from her when I admitted what I'd done.

The next day, she went down to the station to try and sort it all out for me. It had been a bit of harmless fun, but actually it was illegal and dangerous and had the potential to get me into a lot of trouble.

She told them that I was joining the marines in just a few weeks and they said they'd take that into account but it was likely I'd have to have my case heard in the youth offender's court.

It wasn't an exciting prospect. I was just starting to pack up my room and belongings in preparation for moving out and into the Navy barracks, and now I wasn't sure if I would be going at all.

It was a tense time.

A week before I was set to leave, I finally received a letter summoning me to see the chief of police in Hexham.

Mam came with me, and when we got there I was given a

proper dressing down. But it soon became apparent I was going to be let off with a warning – all because I was joining the marines.

They told me to expect far worse reprimands from my commanding officers, and said I would need to grow up fast if I was going to make it through basic training. 'If you put one foot wrong there, they'll sort you out,' I was told.

Presumably they were thinking that the marines would knock any bad behaviour out of me, so there was no point in them disciplining me.

I was very lucky, and Mam couldn't believe it. Neither could I to be honest. It was a close call.

Finally, it was nearly time for me to leave Prudhoe: I had one more night before I boarded the train to Lympstone – for good.

I said goodbye to my grandad, who wished me luck. He'd wanted to join the army himself as a teen, but couldn't because he was colour-blind. He was proud I was doing it instead.

I went to see all my mates, who told me to 'smash it', and then went over to Laura's house to say goodbye to her.

We'd agreed that it made sense to break up for the time being, so it was a sad few hours. I had appreciated her honesty when she told me: 'I don't think I can do this – it's too far and I'm never going to see you.'

But although I knew it was the right thing to do I would still miss her. We'd been together for over a year – that's a lifetime when you're a teenager. I remember standing at her back door as she cried her eyes out and told me she loved me. I was devastated, and when she handed me a card she'd made me I found it hard to hold back the tears myself.

This was it – I was leaving my whole world. I had a good life, but I wanted more. And to get it, I'd have to sacrifice everything I knew.

The next morning, Mam tried to stay strong as she dropped me off at the train station. She hugged me tight and told me to stay in touch. I promised her I would, and tried to reassure her that I would be fine.

But as the train pulled into the station, I picked up my bag and thought: 'Shit: this is it. I'm 16 and I'm moving out. I'm going to train with huge lads, older lads, and, in essence, prepare for war. What the hell am I doing?'

PARSNIP POINTERS

NO. 4: THE COCKBLOCK

Sometimes a friend is still hanging around at the end of the night – even if you've followed the 'Sealing the Deal' rules perfectly. It happens when the girl you've got your eye on has a mate that just won't leave her alone. This can be fatal to your sex life.

Friends are pretty awesome at cockblocking.

On nights out, the rule is always bros before hoes and chicks before dicks, depending on your gender. This is all well and good. Mates are more important than a shag in the long-term. But it does make for a bit of awkwardness when they're getting in the way of you getting some action.

Don't worry. There is still hope for your parsnip yet.

Invite them both back for a few drinks at your place. The night is young, you say, let's carry on the party at home. Everyone feels welcome, everyone feels safe – it's a ball ache for you, but it'll be worth it if you pull it off.

When you get home, sneak off and call a taxi, asking for it to arrive in 45 minutes. Tell both of the girls you'll make sure they get home safely a little later. This is going to be a long and frustrating 45 minutes, but stay strong.

The parsnip will thank you for your strength of character.

Pour the drinks, have a laugh, ask her friend to tell you about herself. Sit closer to the girl you want and try to make sure you have some kind of skin-to-skin contact so she knows you're interested. She'll start to get horny, and frustrated because her friend is there. And even better, you're still acting all interested in chatting to her friend, which makes her want you even more.

When the taxi arrives, act laid-back about it. But when you go to kiss your chosen girl goodbye, tell her you wish she could stay.

Look genuine and innocent. As if you wouldn't dream of taking her away from her friend, however much you like her.

This makes it clear you want her but doesn't offend her mate, who should, with any luck, give you her blessing and tell her mate to stay and have a good time.

She knows where you live, she knows her mate will be safe with you, she thinks you're a sound lad – now the girl you really want has nothing to stop her from staying if she wants to.

IN THE NAVY

The friend leaves happy, and, as soon as you're alone, it's game on. She'll have a great story to tell her mate the next day.

CHAPTER 5

DILEMMAS AND DEAD ENDS

When the train pulled into Lympstone, all I could see was uniformed marines, everywhere. No one slouched, no one hung around, aimlessly – and everyone was neatly turned out.

Welcome to the armed forces.

I gathered with all the new recruits for our initial briefing, before being sent straight to the barbers to have my carefully gelled spikes shaved off.

It's literally the first thing they do when you join – give you a buzz cut. They say it's for hygiene purposes, and to make it quicker and easier to get ready in the morning, as you don't have a lot of time for personal care when you're fighting a war.

But it's also part of their training regime. They strip everyone down before they remould them into fighting machines, and having the same haircut as everyone else is the first stage of training. It helps them to see you not as an individual, but as a part of a group. And it helps you see it that way too – you're only as good as your whole team. No one person is more important than the group.

It would be what helped me stay alive if I ever went to war, but it was also this mindset that I began to have problems with. I wanted to be an individual. I was always trying to stand out from the crowd. But in the marines that wasn't really how things worked. I'd have to come to terms with it somehow, or I wouldn't make it.

Next we were issued with our kit. Every single item of clothing was military issue, and we all looked exactly the same by the end of the very first day.

My troop was the 886 division, and we quickly got stuck into training together. Everyone was buzzing, excited to learn so much and to be trained so hard.

On the first day all we really did was a bit of training in the gym, so that the instructors could see how fit we were. And for the rest of the week we settled into our new routines.

Each day we got up at 5am, made our beds, got changed and had drill lessons. This was to teach us to march properly as a troop, which is a lot harder than it looks.

We were also taught the basics, like ironing and polishing our boots – in exactly the same way as everyone else. It was all very strict, and there was a lot of yelling. But that never bothered me. It wasn't a surprise, as I knew that was how they did things. But some lads would literally be quaking in their boots once the drill sergeant started screaming in their faces.

It felt strange bedding down with 50 other lads in a dormitory. All our belongings had to fit in our bedside lockers, and these had to be neat and orderly at every single inspection.

I quickly excelled in the fitness side of things, and my scores were consistently high. We were shown how to make our webbing and put up our bivvys, which would be our shelter on overnight expeditions, and I was a quick learner.

The regular camp circuit run was a 900-metre uphill dash that had to be completed in under three minutes – in all weather conditions. I loved it.

After a few weeks we also got to get our hands on a rifle for training, which was much more fun than polishing our boots, over and over again.

We learnt how to wash ourselves in the field, cook food and set up sentry positions. We had extensive training in the water, which I didn't find hard because I'd always been a good swimmer.

And we had lectures on fieldcraft, map reading and strategy and tactics, and it was fascinating to really see how expeditions were organised. We also learned first aid so that we could help our fellow marines if necessary, and all the while our fitness was getting better and better due to the countless hours we had to spend in the gym and the miles of running we did outside.

We did have time off, but there wasn't really much to do, so it was really boring. I preferred being in training to be honest, as at least you were doing something to take your mind off missing your family and friends.

Although I loved the fitness and the lessons, I struggled with the lifestyle. I got the third highest assault course time in my troop, but I just couldn't get my head around the perfection we had to show in every single little thing we did.

After a few weeks I was really confused at how I was feeling. I'd really wanted this, and now I was beginning to have severe doubts – should I leave? Could I leave? What would I do if I left?

You have to really love the life to have a career in the armed forces. And although it had only been a few weeks, I knew I really didn't. Did I want this for the next two years of my life? I wasn't sure at all.

Soon after, I called Mam for a chat. I told her that I wasn't failing, but that I really didn't like it, and she told me to leave if I felt that way.

'I'm sorry mate,' I eventually told Scott, who was loving the regimental routine of it all. 'I'm going to have to try and leave.'

He understood. I wasn't the first to go – other lads had been pulling out regularly as the weeks had passed – and he didn't make me feel like I couldn't hack it.

At least I wasn't failing. Lots of the lads simply weren't fit enough and were being kicked out because of it.

But it isn't all about fitness. It's about a mindset too, and I just didn't have the right one. Like I've already said, I saw myself as an individual. I wanted to be noticed, not just one lad in a long line of people who all walked, talked and acted the same way. I wanted to be my own person, and be the best possible version of who I was, but they just wanted me to be exactly like everyone else there. There was no room for individuality. I couldn't shine. It wasn't for me.

And so I went and spoke to the powers-that-be, and eventually they said I could leave. I was too young, I told them. It just wasn't for me at the moment.

I didn't want to feel like a failure, but I had to go. I just wanted to be back home, although I had no idea what I would do when I got there. All my mates were doing their A-levels and I couldn't just join them – I'd have to wait a year before I started any college course.

I tried not to think about it. I just wanted out.

On the morning I was due to leave, I got changed into my old jeans and T-shirt and handed back all my kit. As I was doing my final packing, the sergeant came in and started screaming at the kid next to me. 'Your bed! What the fuck has happened to your bed! Get down now!'

The kid quickly lowered himself into the press-up position and there he stayed. The sergeant took his time inspecting every other bed in the dorm, while this lad was sweating with the effort of staying upright, with his arms straining to hold him in position, shaking like a leaf.

I whispered: 'Why don't you just leave?'

He replied: 'I can't. This is my second attempt. I'm here for good this time.'

You could leave once, with the option of returning. But if you came back, you were in it for the long haul.

I told him I was off and he said: 'Fuck you, you lucky bastard.'

On the train back home, all I felt was relief. When I arrived, Mam threw her arms around me and said it was a dream come true that I'd returned. Her boy was back and he wasn't going anywhere for a long while.

Then I went up to my room, which still had my old Newcastle United wallpaper on the walls, and flopped down on my own bed.

I slept well for the first time in a month.

PARSNIP POINTERS

NO. 5: NEGGING

Some girls, especially the really fit and over-confident ones, are so used to being showered with compliments that you need to try a radically different approach to get them to go home with you. This is where the art of negging comes in.

Negging takes a lot of practice and a careful touch. You have to be in tune as to whether a girl will respond to a neg, and even then you have to gauge how heavy a neg to drop into the conversation.

Negging is basically where you say something a little bit mean to show her you're different and get her passions fired up. It's a bit like pulling a girl's hair in the playground at school.

She's spent hours getting herself all dolled up to go out and won't be expecting anyone to criticise her appearance – she's just not used to it. So the shock of your neg will catch her interest. Then she'll see it as a challenge to get you to say something nice about her, which means you can have a conversation.

A neg can be anything from telling her that her roots need doing, to asking whether she meant to choose those shoes or did she just run out of time getting ready.

If she tells you she is a model, you can say something like: 'What, a hand model?'

Or you can tell her that there is something in her hair and reach out to remove it, before recoiling, looking a bit disgusted, and saying: 'Nah, you'd better do it yourself actually…'

For added effect, give your hands a little wipe on your top too.

It's all about playfully and accidentally letting her know that you're not going to fawn all over her like every other guy that's already come up to her to try it on. You're different. Girls like a guy who's different.

CHAPTER 6

TRADING PLACES

After the excitement of being back home had worn off, reality kicked in and once more I found myself wondering what the heck I was going to do with my life.

I began looking for a job to tide me over, and I ended up working in a call centre for Northern Rock. It was all right really. I was advising people on what to do with their savings, so it was all maths-based work. I had to wear a suit and tie and it was very different to what I had been used to. But at least I could be myself, and it gave me a good insight into what to do with my finances when I finally had some cash to my name.

Having money would be all well and good, and I was determined to somehow earn myself a comfortable living. But once I had any real money behind me I knew I wouldn't just keep it in a bank account, doing nothing. I planned to be much cleverer than that with my earnings.

The other good thing about Northern Rock was the fit

birds, who were all dressed in sexy secretary-style outfits. I felt like a kid in a sweet shop.

I'd walk around the office, getting the names of the ones I liked from their name badges, and then email them all, one by one.

'Hey how are you,' I'd begin. 'How long have you been here? I've only just started...'

I never came on too strong, I just got to know them over email and then moved on to some cheeky light-hearted flirting. I'd see them giggling away behind their desks, and I knew I was onto a sure thing.

After a few days I nearly got busted, when my manager came over and perched on the end of my desk. 'You do realise,' he said, trying to hide a grin, 'that I get a copy of every single email you send?'

So I stuck to getting their numbers from then on.

I hooked up with Nicky Kerr again, and finally began to drink alcohol. I wasn't playing serious football anymore, I wasn't in the marines – I couldn't see a reason not to have a drink or two. I hated beer, so I always stuck to spirits: vodka especially.

We started drinking at the pubs in Prudhoe – local watering holes that everyone used to go to.

Since I was now single, I gave my full attention to a stream of girls from the area and, after a long hiatus, started to try and catch Nicky up again. It was good to be back with my mates, and I quickly felt settled in my little world once more.

Everyone was out drinking and having fun together, and there were plenty of girls to keep me occupied. My job wasn't hard and I kind of enjoyed it – I felt like I was in a period of transition, but not one that was tough. It was all good.

One night we all went out to celebrate a mate's birthday in Prudhoe. His name was Mark and he would be turning 18 at midnight, so me, Nicky and the lads were giving him an early party.

I had a few drinks but nothing mad. I was only just starting to get a taste for booze, so I never really went over the top. I went home at half ten and told Mark I'd call him in the morning, as we'd arranged to go shopping to buy some new threads for his proper birthday do the next day.

Everyone else carried on drinking. They were just starting to line up shots on the bar as I left...

The next morning, I called Mark's house and his dad answered.

'Is Mark there?' I asked casually, wondering if he was still in bed with a hangover.

His dad's voice sounded odd when he replied: 'No, he's not.'

'Oh,' I said. 'Where is he?'

'Gaz,' he said gently and with great difficulty. 'He's dead.'

I couldn't understand what he was telling me – was this some kind of bad joke? But as I heard the sound of sobbing begin at the other end of the telephone, it quickly became clear it wasn't.

What he told me next truly broke my heart.

Apparently Mark had enjoyed a variety of shots the night before, necking anything that was put in front of him as quickly as possible.

It was a rite of passage I guess – everyone gets plastered on their 18th. But not everyone realises how dangerous it can be.

He had been staggering drunk by the time he left the pub, and had even fallen over when he got outside. But he made it into someone's car and was driven home safely.

His dad had put him to bed to sleep it off, but he just never woke up. He'd been found the next morning, stone cold in his bedroom. He'd drunk too much, too quickly, and it had shut down his system and killed him.

It hit me so hard. I'd never known anyone my age to die before and I couldn't understand how it had happened. It was such a waste of a life. Mark had been funny and kind – a good lad. He didn't deserve to die.

We weren't massive drinkers either, so it didn't seem possible that he'd died from boozing. He had left three little brothers behind, who had all looked up to him, and his family was broken.

Everyone in Prudhoe was shocked. In such a small town it was a huge deal. When I put the phone down after talking to his dad I immediately called my mate Ben Anick, a goalkeeper for Sunderland. He was on his way to training and he said: 'Are you taking the piss?'

No one could believe it. It was a random, tragic, shocking event, which took me years to get over and taught me a lot.

You will never see me so drunk that I can't walk, so drunk that I don't know what I am doing. I've already said that I like to be in control, and Mark's death confirmed to me that while drinking was fun, it was dangerous to be out of control.

It can kill you.

I drink a lot, but I'll never be so plastered that I can't get myself into a taxi. I'll never be so drunk that I'm practically comatose on the floor, vomiting.

I know my limits and I will always stick to them.

And now, whenever I see people who are very drunk, I always think of Mark and do whatever I can to help. On *Geordie Shore*, you'll see that if the girls have had a few too many, I often help them home, or put them to bed and make sure they're okay.

It's because I care about them, obviously, but it's also because of Mark and what happened to him. I never want that to happen again.

Soon after, on my 17th birthday, I sat my theory test, passed it, and booked my driving test for three weeks later. During that time I had a few lessons just to be sure, but I wasn't worried about passing – I knew I could drive.

As predicted, I passed first time, and used my savings to buy myself a Citroen Saxo, VTR, in dark blue. It was a nippy little machine and it gave me the freedom I had been longing for.

I could go anywhere, at any time, and it was amazing. But although I now had a vehicle, I still didn't have any real destination in mind – for my life anyway. I was working in a bank and while it wasn't bad, I knew I wanted more. I just didn't know what.

During that fallow year, I put any concerns over my future to the back of my mind, and tried to enjoy myself. I had cash, I had a car, I had a roof over my head. Everything would be fine.

And with money to spare, I even booked my first lads' holiday.

Throughout my teenage years I'd gone to Tenerife twice a year with my family. As I'd got older, I'd spent more and more time with the girls and mates I met while on holiday, and less time with Mam and Claire by the pool. It was only natural.

Mam would give me lots of freedom – she'd say I had to be in by 1am and I'd go off and pull girls and maybe even have a drink or two and then sneak back in while she was asleep.

I'm ashamed to say I did cheat on Laura on those holidays.

It was because I was a teenager, pretending to be an adult. I loved her in a teenage way, but looking back it can't have been true love or else I wouldn't have messed about on holiday.

I learned a lot about girls on those holidays. I even fingered my first girl on one of those trips. Years later, after I'd become famous, I did a personal appearance at a Tiger Tiger bar. I'd been in there just minutes when the manager came rushing over and said: 'Gaz, what the fuck has happened?'

The manager was that first girl, whom I'd been with all those years ago.

'This is so weird. I see you on TV and I've known you since we met on that holiday,' she said.

I just laughed. 'Try being me,' I told her.

Since then I've bumped into loads of the girls I met back then – it's a really small world. This is yet another reason to be nice to the girls you pull. You never know when you're going to run into them again.

I remember there was one Tenerife holiday where I was after two girls, who were both called Lyndsey. I called them Lyndsey pink and Lyndsey blue after the swimsuits they were wearing. They were on holiday together. I think I shagged Lyndsey pink... or was it Lyndsey blue?

Honestly, I can't exactly remember. I probably shagged both of them.

But although I had a lot of freedom on my family hols, I still felt like I was sneaking around – probably because I was – and I just wanted to be able to do whatever I liked.

I was making a steady grand a month at the bank, which wasn't bad considering I had no outgoings, and I could afford to take a holiday. Along with my mates Carl Lee and Andy Reay from Prudhoe, I booked a week in Magaluf.

It was messy. A proper 'Inbetweeners' style holiday. Carl was a prolific shagger, like me, and we all decided that it was our mission to shag as many girls as possible.

All the lasses were tanned, wearing tiny bikinis and getting plastered, so it wasn't difficult. But I cringe when I think of how I dressed back then. Tight pink T-shirts, cream jeans, plimsolls – I thought I looked cool, like a proper player, but I just looked like an idiot.

Fortunately it didn't affect my chances with the lasses.

I did well on that holiday.

We went out every single night and managed to pull at least a girl a night. There were girls from all over the UK, all on holiday, all losing their inhibitions for a week. It was bliss.

I snogged my way down the club strip, and back up again, and with no one waiting for me at my hotel I stayed out all night – sometimes taking girls down to the beach for a quickie in the moonlight.

And I remember meeting one girl on the first night who blew me away. She was ridiculously hot and I didn't manage to get her number or anything, so every night from then while I was out I'd look for her.

My mates thought it was hilarious and would often point to a girl and say: 'There she... isn't!'

But I was determined to find her, and on the very last night I finally spotted her. I caught her eye again and we got chatting. One thing led to another and I got her back to my hotel room.

Lying on the bed, she told me: 'I'm a virgin.'

I stopped what I was doing and looked her in the eye. It was a big deal: I wanted to make sure she was ready. It wouldn't be fair for me to just fuck her, when for her it would be something she remembered for the rest of her life.

GAZ (AND MY PARSNIP)

I'm not trying to big myself up – it wouldn't be anything to do with me personally, but you always remember your first time. I didn't want to be responsible for ruining what should be a unique experience for someone if they weren't ready.

'Are you sure you want to do this?' I asked.

'There's no one back home,' she replied. 'Yes I want to!'

I sincerely hope that I made it special for her.

When I got back, it was time to start thinking seriously about my life. Summer was coming to an end, which meant September was on its way and if I wanted to go back to school or do some kind of course I had to start applying quickly.

My mate Nicky Kerr was by now in his third year of an apprenticeship to be a joiner and was making £300–400 a week. He was always flush and drove a nice car.

Another mate who was in another trade was making £700 a week – it was big money and I wanted in on the action. So I applied for an apprenticeship with a company called Plunkett's Tiling.

I would be at college for two weeks, and working with Plunkett's for the other two weeks of the month. It would be a huge pay cut at first – apprentices only make £150 a week.

But it seemed like a good mix of study and work, and when I passed my three-year course I could set myself up as a tiler and rake in the cash. I wasn't really that excited about tiling, but it was a trade and I needed to do something.

Mam agreed. 'You can sit in a bank, getting a grand a month and in five years' time you could still be on that,' she said. 'Get a trade and at first you may be a bit skint, but in a few years you'll be sorted.'

I nailed the interview and got ready to start at Ashington College in September.

NO. 6: THE ICE CUBE GAME

This is the easiest way on the planet to pull a bird. Me and Scott used it in Amsterdam and it always works like a charm.

All you need is a couple of ice cubes and a lot of girls. Basically you put the ice cube in your mouth and kiss a girl to pass it on to them. They pass it on, you kiss the next girl to take it off her. On and on it goes until you've snogged all of them and the ice cube is gone.

It's a mint excuse to watch other girls kiss and a legitimate reason to snog the face off a load of girls in a row.

Kissing gets them all hot and bothered. They're guaranteed to want more. All you have to do now is take one off for a one-on-one game and you're in.

Kissing is an international language. This game works in every country.

CHAPTER 7

NEWCASTLE COMES CALLING

I strolled into Ashington college on my first day thinking I was the man. This wasn't school, as such, so I wasn't worried about making friends. We were all in the same boat, right? We'd just get on with our study and learn our trades.

Wrong.

'Ha, you fucking mincer!' said one lad, pointing at me as I sat down at my new desk. I looked around at all the lads, who were staring and laughing at my pink T-shirt and plimsolls.

They were rough.

Don't get me wrong, as it turned out they were good lads – I'm still mates with some of them now – but in those first few weeks I got bullied mercilessly by the whole class, who were, quite frankly, a bunch of chavs.

I was clean cut and wore designer labels, while they were rough diamonds, not used to my middle-class kind. Plus I didn't have the safety net of a football team to join to be instantly cool.

It was going to be a challenge, but I was up for it. I just had to figure out how to make myself liked.

The top dog in the class was a lad called Mickey. Everyone was a bit scared of this guy and no one would stand up to him. He was a big lad, covered in scars and obviously wasn't afraid of a fight.

I knew he would be my ticket to popularity.

So I started being cheeky to him to get a bit of banter going between us. It was a risk – some of the things I said to him, I swear I was expecting a slap for. But somehow I got away with it. He thought I was funny and eventually we became mates.

We were a motley bunch, but though we were all from different backgrounds we got on well. Along with Mickey there were three other lads – Steve, Daryl and Alex.

I managed to win them all over and although at the beginning they all laughed at me for taking care of my appearance, by the end of the course they were all asking me for advice on outfits.

They'd be like: 'Gaz, we're going to Whitley Bay for a weekend – what shall we wear?'

I would say: 'Oh so now you want my advice – you've changed!'

Mickey was hard and always had a story to tell after the weekend. 'Five lads were on us,' he'd say. 'Throwing bottles at my head.'

I was shocked. 'Where do you live, man? I go out pulling at the weekend, you come back with new scars.'

He'd shake his head. 'It's rough where I live.'

He lived in the Arcades, where he was known for having the hardest punch for miles around. While I was knocking about with lasses in the suburbs, Mickey was out in the most dangerous parts of Newcastle. It was frightening to hear about his life. I was certainly glad he was my mate and not my enemy.

Times were good in that first year. I upgraded my car to a baby blue mini, and Mam even bought me a personalised number plate for it for Christmas. I've still got it on the Ferrari I drive today.

It was in those years that I really started going out partying. At first I stayed in Prudhoe, going out on weekdays as well as weekends and constantly turning up for work or college with a raging hangover.

I perfected my pulling techniques and realised that while some girls I could get into bed on the first night, others would take a week or even a month of chatting up. It was hard graft, but I didn't mind putting in the hours to get all the girls I wanted.

I even kind of enjoyed the tiling work.

On my first job I didn't even know what it was I was supposed to be doing. I arrived with my pristine little kit to tile a bus station in Stanley with this guy called John Bainbridge.

He'd been a tiler for 20 years, and his son had followed him into the trade. We were there for a few weeks and I loved hearing all of their mad stories as we got on with the work.

As my 18th birthday approached, I began getting restless. I knew everyone in Prudhoe, had shagged most of the girls there and was bored with the pubs, which were fairly quiet and all closed early.

Lots of people I knew from college were going out in Newcastle, and it sounded like much more fun.

So for my 18th, I told everyone I wanted a night out in the Big City. I got myself primped and preened and travelled into Newcastle to celebrate my coming of age.

It was mad – a real eye-opener. The bars were huge, the clubs were packed and there were girls everywhere. Hundreds of girls I'd never met, all wearing teeny tops and even tinier skirts.

I was used to local pubs – this was another world and I loved it. It was like being on holiday and I slept with my 50th bird that night. I like to think it was a fitting way to mark the occasion.

The next weekend, all my mates were having their usual conversation: 'Where shall we go out?'

I just said: 'I don't know where you guys are off to but I'm going to Newcastle again...'

From then on the city was my new playground, and I went out almost every night. Claire's, Sam Jacks, Liquid, The Mushroom – the clubs were immense and I couldn't get enough of them.

I'd always get told off for being hungover or late for work but I didn't care. I was in heaven. Nicky would join me, and I met a load of new lads from Newcastle too.

I stuck to my usual pulling technique, which was essentially a more adult version of pulling a girl's pigtails in the playground.

I'd make eye contact, then go up to them and say something like: 'What the hell are you wearing on your feet?'

They'd all look a bit taken aback and say something like: 'What do you mean? They're nice shoes!'

I'd roll my eyes. 'Yeah, yeah. You keep telling yourself that, love.' Then I'd walk off. They'd always follow. Then I'd buy them a drink and ask them for a kiss. I was never a smoothie, I was always a cheeky so-and-so. And it always worked for me.

They were good years, and I soon got a name for myself as a man about town. I knew all the club promoters and dancers and our group of lads were well known.

There was Nicky, obviously, but also Michael Bowman, Graham Minto, Darren Guttridge and Callum Collbeck.

Minto was a builder, Bowman a joiner like Nicky, and Callum worked at Northern Rock.

We were a proper bunch of Likely Lads.

Another lad who was big on the scene was my mate BJ – Michael Pooley. He lived in town, so I'd take girls back to his place to shag them. Together we were legendary.

I just loved going out. I never got bored of it. It was mint hanging out with the lads and chasing all the women. Even now I love walking into a club and feeling the music thunder through me. Everyone's in a good mood, everyone is up and dancing and you're surrounded by a constant stream of lasses – it's wicked.

Of course I did see people scrapping but we weren't fighting lads. We just loved the girls and the booze and the partying. Punching or getting punched wasn't on our agenda.

I didn't want to be a Mickey – the lad from my college course. I thought he was mint, but he was completely different to me. For him, it was normal to get into scraps, whether it was to defend himself or whatever, but I couldn't imagine anything worse.

This was confirmed to me at the end of my first year at college.

I walked into class one day and there was an empty chair where Mickey usually sat. 'Where is he?' I asked, wondering if he was hungover or late. But the lads looked ashen-faced.

'Gaz, he killed someone on Saturday night,' one of them said. 'He's in prison.'

Killed someone? Mickey? It didn't seem possible. He was a little bit rough, but he was a good lad – a nice lad.

What on earth had happened?

Eventually I heard the full story: he had been out with his girlfriend and this group of lads had been winding him up, throwing chips at his lady's head. Mickey had told them to pack it in, but they were pissed and wouldn't stop messing around. Eventually Mickey had thrown a warning punch at the ringleader – just one, solitary punch.

But this was the guy with the hardest punch in Newcastle.

The poor lad was dead before he hit the floor.

He hadn't meant to kill him. But drunken fights can have dangerous consequences. And for Mickey that meant five years in prison.

I was devastated – he was my best mate in college and it was a tragedy. Mickey was protecting his girlfriend from the silly antics of a pissed-up lad who didn't know any better – but it had ended up with one guy dead and another in prison.

It seemed so unnecessary: why fight?

So I made doubly sure I stayed away from any altercation from then on. People could be right numpties when they were pissed up. It just wasn't worth it. I'd rather keep the peace and walk away than start a punch-up.

This was yet another reason to keep my wits about me on nights out, and reminded me once again not to get so smashed that I didn't know what I was doing. One of my mates was dead and now another was in prison – all because of too much booze.

It was a sober reminder to stay grounded. My advice is to

enjoy nights out, by all means – I certainly did back then and still do today. But always keep control of yourself. You just never know what's going to happen.

Somehow, while partying nearly every night of the week, I got through my three-year apprenticeship.

I learnt my trade and did tiling jobs all over the place – including at the Metrocentre, the biggest shopping 'mall' in the UK.

That was a huge job, which was mostly done at night and took years to finish. We had to retile the whole place and the job felt never-ending.

I hated it. Night after night I'd take my tools and go to work next to all these shops – there are over 300 of them – that saw thousands of pounds go through their cash registers every single day. I felt like some kind of skivvy. I was late for work all the time. I'd wake up on a Wednesday morning and remember that my car was at some random bird's house and I had to go get it. Not good.

Back then I used every excuse I could think of for being late on site, and I was given hundreds of warnings. It started to get really dull, and I wasn't enthusiastic about spending my whole life on building sites. I was only an apprentice and already I'd heard the older guys tell me the same boring tiling story a hundred times over.

Bless them, they were good guys. But I found it hard.

Every day on site the guy next to me would eat the same cheese-and-pickle sandwich he'd eaten for the two years I'd known him. I'd wake up each Monday morning and feel sick of my life.

I'd think: 'I've spent all my money boozing again, and now I've got to grout four bathrooms. What am I doing?'

But it was a means to an end and I hoped once I was on better money I'd enjoy it more. And at least I was getting a name for myself on the Newcastle clubbing scene.

I finally finished my apprenticeship and became a fully qualified tiler for Plunkett's. But for me it was no real cause for celebration. I hated it.

A few days into my newly qualified role, I was late on site – again. I'd had a sober night out for once and was staying round a mate's house.

He'd left for work, and I followed soon after – but when I got to my car I realised I'd left the stupid keys inside his flat and I couldn't get back in to get them.

I had to get Mam to bring round the spare car keys from home and by the time I got to the building site I was half an hour late.

It was the last straw: I was sacked on the spot.

All that work doing an apprenticeship and now I didn't even have a job. It was my fault, but I felt like it had all been for nothing.

I really began to drift.

PARSNIP POINTERS

NO. 7: COLD CALLING

When you spot a girl in a club and you want to talk to her, don't just go over unannounced. You have no idea if she's interested and the last thing you want is to get pied.

It'll knock your confidence and set you back for the rest of the evening.

You need to get to know her before you even say a word. It's all about eye contact. Look at her and catch her eye. Look away, look back, see if she's checking you out, give her a little smile…

You'll be able to tell if she's interested at all by her actions. If she keeps looking at you, and maybe gives you a smile back, that's the green light to go over.

If she turns her back to you, don't even bother approaching her. The parsnip does not want to get pied in public.

CHAPTER 8

MINT TIMES IN MALIA

Feeling sick of everything, I decided I needed a change. I moved out of my family home and went to live with a lad called John Reay, who owned a three-storey town house in Newcastle's city centre.

He was my age but had done really well for himself work-wise and was already on the property ladder.

John was a player too, and when we got together there was no stopping us. We competed with each other to get as many birds as possible and started a huge game of one-upmanship.

I had a laptop and we set up a spreadsheet to record our scores, even going as far as devising a points system for fairness.

We had a camera on the windowsill upstairs and, when you said goodbye to a lass at the door, you had to sprint up and take a picture of them getting into a taxi as proof of your night. We put the pics in an album and thought it was hilarious: picture after picture of the same scene at different times of the day and with different girls. The taxis were all parked in the same place, and each shot had a different coloured cab in it. That album was our most prized possession.

After losing my job I'd signed on, and so by now I was on the dole. I spent all my benefit money on going out and eventually I was so skint that I'd have to take pound coins from a jar John used to keep his change in and sneak down to KFC to get a meal.

It was pretty awful, and for the first time Mam got on my case about finding a job. She didn't like seeing me waste my life away, even if for me it had the benefit that I could suffer through my raging hangovers without having to get up for work.

As a temporary fix, a mate of mine got me a job selling cars at a garage in Newcastle. I thought it was easy – selling was so similar to pulling birds. Instead of selling myself I was selling motors. I'd flirt a little, chat up the customer, and hey presto – I'd get £100 commission.

I also spent a lot of time with my mate Tez – Terry Mitchell. We'd met in Newcastle when I was 18 and just starting to go clubbing. I'd lost all my mates one night, probably because I was chasing some girl, and so I was just at the bar having a drink and wondering what to do next. He came and stood next to me and asked me what was happening. I told him I'd lost my pals and he said he had too.

'Shall we get a bottle of sambuca and get smashed?' I asked.

'I can't really afford it mate,' he'd laughed.

'Neither can I,' I shrugged. 'Fuck it, let's do it anyway.'

We were close from that moment on, and while I was living with John he was always around for nights out.

But by the time the next summer came round I was bored again. So I made another decision – I was off to party in sunnier climes.

I literally had £150 to my name when I decided to book a trip to Malia – a well-known party destination that was luckily also very cheap. It was £99 for a week's stay, which was a rock-bottom price that I could just about afford.

My mate Bowman decided to come along with me. But while he was planning on going back to Newcastle at the end of the week, I wasn't. I wanted to stay out there and work.

I didn't really have a clue how, or if it was even possible, but I thought I'd leave it up to fate to decide. If I got a job, great; if not, I'd come back and make a new plan. I had no responsibilities, no ties – there was nothing stopping me doing whatever I wanted.

The day before I left for Malia, I went and had a drink with my former mentor, Nicky. By now he'd settled down with a lass and was all loved-up. I was pleased for him. Especially since it had given me a chance to catch up with him in the shagging stakes. He'd always been so far ahead, but now I had some news for him…

'What are you on now, Nicky?' I asked, casually.

He laughed and said: 'I'm out of the game, son. Final score: 122.'

'I've caught you up, matey,' I grinned. I was on 157.

'And guess where I'm going tomorrow?' I added, rubbing it in. 'Malia!'

He said: 'Fuck me', and slapped me on the back. After all those years of being his little apprentice, I'd finally done him proud.

When I arrived in Malia, a coastal town on the paradise

island of Crete, I actually felt like I'd found heaven. Yes, I only had a few quid to my name and could only afford to eat Pot Noodles all week. But the weather was perfect, the booze was cheap, and the girls – well the girls were everywhere.

I couldn't afford to buy many drinks on our evenings out, but we'd buy a cheap bottle of vodka every night and get smashed before we hit the strip.

The place was mint. Like I've said before, pulling girls on holiday is so easy. You get them in the pool, brush up past them underwater and you're already halfway to getting them back to your bedroom.

At night, everyone is out for the same reason – to get drunk and pull – so if you played your cards right you could pull whenever you liked. I definitely knew the right way to play my cards.

As the end of the week approached, I knew I couldn't go home. Malia was the perfect place for me, and working there would be one long party. I asked around and lined up a job PR-ing at a place called The Help Bar – chatting up the girls to entice them into the place.

Bowman wished me luck and flew home to Newcastle. With my holiday technically over I now had nowhere to stay. For the first few days, I literally had to pull to make sure I had a bed for the night. I also often slept on a sofa belonging to the bar manager who had given me my job. It was a transient existence but I didn't care.

My hours were 10pm till 3am, and I made 40 euros a night. It was plenty of money to keep me going over the summer, and that's all I was looking for.

While I learned the ropes, back home all my mates had been

amazed to learn that I wasn't coming back. So they all came out en masse to party with me for two weeks.

I met up with them every night after work and it felt like I was just on one long holiday. Even at the bar it didn't really feel like I was working. I fitted in perfectly with the summer working crowd, and soon began making a name for myself on the strip as a ladies' man.

When my Newcastle mates finally said goodbye, I rented myself a little scooter and settled into my new life. I hung around with the summer workers, who all knew each other, and learnt where everyone went on their days off and what life was like on the island.

I got friendly with a lad called Billy Clark who was a PR guy too, and after just a few days he told me he was moving in with a lad called Max and needed a third roomie.

'I've heard about the damage you're doing with the ladies,' he laughed. 'Why don't you move in with us?'

It wasn't The Ritz, but it was mint. We only had one bedroom, with three beds laid out in it, and it looked like a school dormitory. But we got on like a house on fire, and when another lad, Rob, moved in, our little gang was complete.

It was the start of one of the best summers of my life. Even now I see it as when I was at my absolute happiest. We wreaked carnage together all season. We'd shag two, three girls a night!

I might pull a girl while I was working, sneak out the back and give her one, then head back inside to do it all over again. Then after work I'd meet up with the lads and we'd go on the prowl together.

Sometimes I'd be shagging and Billy would walk in, give me a huge thumbs up, and walk straight back out again. Other times we'd all be shagging different girls in our beds at the same time.

We had competitions amongst ourselves to keep up the banter – it was like one huge game, and we never ran out of women. Every week a new wave of girls would arrive to replace the ones who were going home, and you never shagged one girl more than a couple of times.

I was mostly at the top of the shagging leader board, but the lads were stiff competition (no pun intended).

We had so much fun. We'd get up, have a three-euro fry-up in a local café, then get on our scooters and head down to the beach. We played footie and lounged around, or scouted for girls to invite to the bars we worked in on the strip – laying the groundwork for pulling them later on. We'd explore the hills and mountains on our bikes during the day, work our shifts at night, and rampage through the strip in the early hours of the morning.

We mostly didn't go to bed until the sun was up.

Billy became one of my closest friends and I didn't have one unhappy moment the whole time I was there.

On Mondays the workers would all get together and do the Malia slide – a whole day of drinking where we let off steam together. I knew every person who worked in every club and bar and we were all like one big family. We were there to make sure that holidaymakers had the best time of their lives, and in order to do that we had to enjoy ourselves too.

I got tanned and fit and felt happier than I had in a long time.

Then, one night towards the end of the season, while I was still wading through the endless stream of women, I saw an absolute bombshell strutting down the strip.

With long blonde hair and a body like Barbie, she turned heads everywhere she went. 'Fuck me,' said one of the lads, his jaw dropping. 'Some lucky bastard will get to tap that.'

Everyone wanted her and had a go at chatting her up. These were all well practised lads, who knew how to convince a girl to kiss them. But Emily – as I later found out she was called – just brushed them all off like flies.

I wanted her. Badly.

The next day I was walking along the beach when I spotted her practically shovelling a hangover burger into her mouth. 'You whale,' I yelled, walking over. 'Look at you, stuffing your face.'

She was so cute, even with a face full of burger, and she tried to speak before she'd even swallowed her mouthful. 'What are you doing?' I teased. 'Talking with your mouth full – really?'

She laughed and I knew I'd broken the ice.

We chatted for a bit and I invited her to the bar I was working at, promising her a few drinks on the house. I knew she would come, I could tell I'd made an impression – but I still couldn't stop looking outside for her as I worked my shift that night.

I didn't even try to work my magic on any of the birds who came in that evening. I was saving all my attention for her. Sure enough, towards the end of the night, in she strutted.

After just a few minutes I knew she was my ideal woman. She was from Birmingham and was on holiday with her mates, she told me. She was single and just wanted to have fun.

Well I was definitely the guy for that.

But not only was she a knockout, she really made me laugh too. She had great banter, was easygoing and sweet, and to be honest she was just about perfect. That night, she agreed to come home with me. I put her on the back of my scooter and drove up and down the strip a few times to show the lads what I'd managed to do.

That's right... I nodded at them as I slowly rolled past. *She's mine...!*

The next day we hung out together. And that night she came home with me again. When I was at work, I couldn't get her out of my head. When we were together, the time just flew by. I was besotted: every time she smiled I found myself smiling back.

For the whole two weeks she was in Malia we spent every moment we could together.

The lads were unimpressed – spending 14 nights with the same girl was unheard of. It was practically against the staff rules. But I felt so differently about Emily. I wanted to really get to know her and I was sad when she finally flew back home.

We promised to keep in touch, and I tried to get back into the swing of things. But although I shagged other girls, my heart wasn't really in it, and my mind kept wandering back to Emily. We texted each other regularly, but she was so far away I didn't think anything else would come of it. I told myself it was just a holiday romance – a relationship made giddy by the sunshine and free-flowing booze.

After three months of living it up in the sun, the season ended and I had to go home.

My shagging total by the end of the summer was 43 birds, taking my grand total up to 200. It would have been so many more if Emily hadn't come along and stopped me in my tracks. I had stormed past Nicky and was surely close to setting a new record in shagging on the Newcastle player scene.

But for now, I was back to square one.

No job, no home, no money, no direction.

It was quickly becoming the story of my life.

NO. 8: BE ON YOUR BEST BEHAVIOUR.

Always be nice to the girl you've pulled. I know lads who have banged a bird and kicked them straight out at 3am. They won't call them a taxi, they won't do anything to help them get home.

That girl will go and tell her mates what a dick he is and word soon gets around.

If you ring them a taxi, be courteous to them, ask if they're okay getting back by themselves and give them cash for a cab… She'll go tell her mates what a nice lad you are, so that when you go out the next week and you see one of her fit mates out on the town, she's already thinking that you're a good guy and you're practically in.

Use the girly gossip network to your own advantage. Don't let it condemn you to going home alone by treating one lass badly once you've got what you want.

CHAPTER 9

ROCK BOTTOM

When I got back from Malia in September 2009, I moved back home with Mam and tried to figure out what my next move should be.

For the next few months, I seriously suffered from the post-holiday blues. One minute my life was one eternal party, the next I was stuck at home, alone, 21 years old, with no idea what to do next. It was a depressing, vicious circle.

I went back on the dole and tried to get a job.

But things were made worse by the fact that I wasn't the only one going through a tough time. Mam had fallen on hard times and was struggling to keep herself afloat. She had broken up with a man she'd been with for a long time, and was very down. She tried to keep it from me, but eventually she had to be honest and admit what was happening.

Not long after after I'd settled back into my childhood bedroom, she had some heartbreaking news for me: she was selling our family home. I was shocked, but she said it was the only way to break even and put her back on track.

I could see she was devastated, and I desperately wished that there was something I could do. I was searching for work but there was nothing out there for me. I had no savings either, so there was nothing I could dip into to prevent her from losing our home. I felt awful. She had worked all her life to pay off the mortgage so that Claire and I would have a good inheritance, and now it was all gone.

She'd given up so much for our family – she had always been there for me and been the best mother I could ever hope for. Now there was nothing I could do to pay her back when she so badly needed someone to step in and help.

We both had to move in with Grandad.

We were both at rock bottom.

Grandad had a big house and was quite happy to have us. Gran had died a few years before and so he was rattling about alone in his big three-bedroom bungalow and said he'd be glad of the company. But although we were grateful, I could tell Mam felt like she'd failed us all.

That Christmas was utterly miserable. No one could afford to buy presents and although Mam still cooked a turkey and tried to make it special I had to give her a hug when she broke down crying halfway through the day.

I told her it didn't matter – that we didn't need presents or a big spread – but you know what mams are like: they want everything to be perfect for their families.

She began driving minibuses for Grandad's company while she figured out what to do next. I stayed at home and watched movies with Grandad, and got addicted to the game *Call of Duty*.

ROCK BOTTOM

At that time I actually got used to being on the dole. I had no drive, no desire to do anything else. I became a completely different person. I wasn't playing football anymore, I wasn't swimming – I was hardly keeping myself fit at all.

I would get up at 10am, saunter down to the gym, come back and play *Call of Duty* with my mate, Bowman.

There was nothing to aim for anymore.

Actually I didn't really feel unhappy at the time, but looking back on it I must have been miserable deep down.

I played that computer game every fucking day for months on end. It was my only focus and as a result I got really good at it. Me and Bowman put together an unbeatable team and even made it into the world leagues.

I thought I was cool but actually I was just doing jack shit and coasting through the days. I cringe when I look back on that time now. I was wasting my time and my life.

Mam started to pick herself up and began to leave the house with a smile on her face again. She'd been driving for a local accountant called George, and she'd impressed him so much with her good nature and her ability to sweet-talk his clients that he offered her a job as his PA.

Everyone has always loved my mam. She is just so genuine and lovely to have around. She started to go away on business trips with George – all around the world. But while she was strolling out of the house with her suitcase every week, I was stretched out on the sofa with my *Call of Duty* headset on.

Mam got a twinkle back in her eye, and soon she began dressing up to go out in the evenings too.

'Where are you off to?' I'd ask.

'Oh, just to the pictures,' she'd reply.

'Who with?' I'd quiz her suspiciously.

'Just George,' she'd say casually.

It wasn't long before I could see that they were falling for each other, and I was happy about it.

George is the kindest, sweetest guy you'll ever meet. He and Mam got married in 2012 and he makes her so happy. They truly deserve each other.

Back then, watching her slowly bloom with love for this new man, I began thinking about how much I wanted that to happen for me too.

And that made me think of Emily – the amazing girl from Malia. We'd kept in touch ever since she'd left the island, and she was still living in Birmingham. Spurred on by seeing how happy Mam was, I invited her up to Newcastle for a weekend.

I couldn't believe it when she said yes.

She drove up and stayed at Grandad's with me. Before she arrived, I admit I was a bit nervous. I wondered if now that we weren't on the steaming hot, booze-laden pleasure island where we'd met, we'd both see each other differently.

I wasn't the sexy club promoter with the best connections on the island, and she wasn't strutting around in a bikini – would the magic still be there?

It was, and more besides. Emily was everything I'd remembered: fun, beautiful, laid-back and a real sweetie.

Mam's first flush of love must have been infectious, because I fell for Emily so quickly I didn't know what had hit me.

We found the same things funny, we laughed all the time and, morning or night, she was stunningly beautiful.

Sometimes when you meet a hot girl on a night out, waking up the next morning next to her can be like being in a horror show. You see the same girl with layers of make-up falling off her face and it's easy to feel you've been duped.

Emily was a natural beauty. Her face didn't need make-up. And she was beautiful on the inside as well as on the outside.

At the end of that first weekend, I told her I wanted to be with her, totally and exclusively. She said she liked me too, and we became a couple.

I was 22, and I had finally settled down.

After that I stopped going clubbing with my mates and did 'couply' things with Emily instead. Every weekend, we took it in turns to visit each other and made the most of our time together by doing really fun things.

I remember early on in our relationship we went away for a spa weekend and decided to go quad biking in the woods surrounding the hotel. Emily got all dolled up and looked amazing. But when we got to the biking area I nearly wet myself laughing – it was off-road, and would be extremely messy. I thought she'd throw a fit, but she just shrugged her shoulders, said 'fuck it', and held on tight.

She gave it her all, in the driving rain, and we flew through the woods covered in dirt. By the end of it she had mud streaked through her hair and all over her face but she didn't care. It was one of the countless moments that confirmed she was special. I felt so proud to be with her.

Back in Birmingham, she had professional footballers after her all the time. They'd turn up at her parents' house in their Bentleys and beg to take her out for dinner.

But she chose me, 22 and on the dole, driving a crappy green VW Golf that I was so ashamed of I had refused to even put my special number plate on it.

She taught me so much about how all that stuff didn't really matter – as long as you were happy, money wasn't important, and for the next year or so that was exactly how I felt.

Because I had Emily and that was all I cared about.

I got a part-time job in a call centre, but I wouldn't say I was committed to it. It was a few hours, a couple of evenings a week, and made me £600 a month. It was just sufficient to fund my visits to Emily, and that was enough for me.

My mate Billy, who I'd met in Malia, moved to Newcastle and was on the dole too. So we spent all week knocking about together, playing on the computer, and then my weekends were filled with Emily.

For over a year, that was my life. It was exhausting, what with all the driving, but it was strangely fulfilling. I was proper loved-up.

Emily and I went on holidays together, and I even went out clubbing with her in the evenings, which was something I'd never done before. Clubbing was for mates and for pulling – not for doing with your girlfriends. It was all new to me but we had so much fun.

On our holidays I quickly discovered that she hated the water and so, because I loved it, I'd always try and entice her in.

One time in Egypt I coaxed her to come swimming and she agreed, but then this massive wave knocked her over, taking her bikini top with it. I had never laughed so much.

The Egyptian men couldn't keep their eyes off her and even offered me 20 camels to buy her from me. Unsurprisingly, no amount of camels could convince me to let her go.

Some nights we would babysit other couples' kids while they went out. We were playing at family life and for the first time I could see myself getting married and having kids with someone. Not just anyone: Emily.

I decided I wanted to marry her, and we discussed taking

things further. We both wanted to, but first we had to sort out the commuting issue, which was wearing us both out. She had a life and a job, while I had neither really, so I started looking into the practicalities of moving to Birmingham. I told Billy that I was deadly serious about her. 'I would propose to her tomorrow if I got a job down there,' I said, wistfully.

I applied for every job going, I didn't care what it was. I'd made up my mind that I was going to do everything I could to make the relationship work, and I had no problem with changing my whole life to do so. But my job applications kept getting rejected.

It was so frustrating. I was ready to move across the country for her, but something kept getting in my way. The months dragged on, with no end in sight for our predicament.

We both still lived with our parents and so we stayed at each other's family homes every weekend. It didn't give us much privacy. And the four-hour drive began to feel like a real chore.

I used to finish work in the call centre at 10pm on a Friday, and hop straight in the car to Birmingham. I'd arrive in the early hours of the morning. We'd wake up together on Saturday mornings and do something fun – like go to a theme park or something. Saturday nights we'd stay in, Sunday we'd chill out and I'd drive back Monday when she went to work.

It couldn't last forever – one of us had to move, or we'd inevitably break up.

Finally, I got a series of job interviews. I went to three and in the last one I got down to the last two applicants. It was an office job, which I'd never been keen on, but I didn't care. I just wanted to move down there, once and for all.

But I didn't get it, and I was devastated.

GAZ (AND MY PARSNIP)

Emily tried to get a transfer to Newcastle with her job, but was turned down too. It felt like the world was against us.

Mam moved in with George and he proposed. I wanted to do the same but we literally couldn't find a way to do it. I felt like my hands were tied. Especially after I'd left the call centre job because it was so dull.

One weekend it all came to a head.

It was Bowman's birthday and so I had to stay in Newcastle and go out with him. 'I'll see you next weekend,' I promised her on the phone.

'I can't,' she said. 'I've got a mate's birthday down here.'

That meant we wouldn't see each other for three weeks, which was far too long. It was a problem we'd been having to face more and more often. We were obviously drifting apart. If we couldn't make time for each other, what were we doing?

'I can't do all this travelling anymore,' I confided in Billy. 'It's just too much.'

I had a tearful conversation with Emily, and we were both honest with each other about the situation. 'I want to see you all the time,' I said. 'It hurts that sometimes it's a month between visits.'

'You haven't got a job and I can't move mine,' she said. 'What can we do?'

We were both sobbing when we eventually agreed to take some time out to figure out what we wanted to do. Deep down we both knew it was over. I was well and truly heart-broken.

When I think about how different my life would be if I'd got a job down in Birmingham, I'm amazed. I'd probably be married to Emily, with a kid on the way.

I'd have been happy, I know I would. I adored her.

ROCK BOTTOM

But it obviously wasn't meant to be.

Because if we hadn't broken up, I wouldn't have been out drinking in Newcastle a few months later when the *Geordie Shore* scouts began scouring the town...

PARSNIP POINTERS

NO. 9: MAKE FRIENDS WITH THE BAR STAFF

Buy whoever is behind the bar a shot at the beginning of the night to get on their good side. Make sure you make eye contact, make small talk, and thank them sincerely for their service.

This will help you get served faster when you want to buy a lass a drink, or if you want to order for her, to be gentlemanly.

Being well connected, especially at a cool club, also makes you look like a big shot, which can only help your chances. Say hello to all the people you know, nod to the bouncers – do everything you can to show that you're not just a barfly but you're a major player on the scene.

Plus there's always a reserve play – you may just end up picking up the barmaid.

CHAPTER 10

SCOUTED

Billy was instrumental in my life during the months that followed my break-up with Emily. I really missed her and felt more than a little bit fragile and broken. Billy was the one who picked me up and put me back together.

He had a dingy little flat in Newcastle and he persuaded me to get back out on the clubbing scene and stay over with him when we went out.

It felt weird at first.

I'd only been out on the town a handful of times in the two years I'd been with Emily. But as the saying goes, it was like riding a town bike – I was back on the booze-and-girls wagon in no time.

I reverted back to the old Gary. I drank, I danced, I pulled. It took my mind off missing Emily, and I quickly rebounded into a relationship with a girl called Carly.

Of course I cared about her a lot, but it was a very different kind of relationship to my last one. We didn't stay in and do cosy, couply things – instead we went out and got smashed together. I wasn't planning a future with her; we were just having fun and it was much more casual than it had been with Emily.

I also still had no money and there's only so far a dole cheque can take you when you're going out every night. I decided I had to sort my life out, so me and Billy both lined up jobs at Sky, in the company's sales department.

We had two weeks of training to suffer through before we could start properly. The job didn't exactly fill me with enthusiasm, but it was something, and that was better than nothing.

I was so broke it was unreal. I'd decided I'd rather be doing work I hated than rooting through my pockets for change for something to eat every day.

The Thursday before the first training week began, Billy called and asked: 'Are we going out tonight?'

I had £20 to my name.

'I can't mate,' I told him. 'I've only got a few quid and I need it for petrol for next week's training.'

But he wouldn't take no for an answer.

'Who cares?' he said. 'Come on, we can buy cheap booze and get our mates to let us into the clubs for free. It'll be fine.'

I wasn't a hard sell. I was in. We spent £8 on the cheapest, nastiest vodka we could find, and drank it before we went out.

Town was absolutely heaving when we started on our regular circuit. I'd heard that some Londoners were out and about, asking questions about the Geordie nightlife for a new TV show they were planning, so I guessed that was the reason. It was good news for me: it meant there were more lasses about and more people to play with. And there was certainly an extra buzz in the air.

Eventually we went to the Tup Tup Palace – one of the biggest nightclubs in the area – and started chatting to a group of lasses.

Out of the corner of my eye I'd spotted two lads and a girl watching us, and in their businesslike, formal clothes they stood out like a sore thumb.

Eventually the girl came over and asked who I was.

'Gary Beadle,' I said, faintly amused. 'Why?'

'Oh so you're Gary,' she said, smiling. 'Your name has popped up a lot tonight.'

'What do you mean?' I asked.

But she ignored the question, and instead said: 'If you were going to chat me up in two seconds, what would you do?'

She had a low-cut top on, and without pausing for thought I grabbed her tits and launched myself at her for a kiss.

'Fucking hell,' said one of the lads with her.

The girl – her name was Lauren – looked shocked, but went with it. 'Okay, she said, composing herself. 'Show me what else you've got.'

It seemed like a fun game, so I strolled over to a random girl, had a little chat with her and got her number. 'Here you go,' I said, handing it to Lauren a few minutes later. 'She had a boyfriend but I got her digits anyway. I'm off now, see you later.'

I strolled off before they could say anything else, working my way through the crowds, saying hi to loads of people I knew and kissing the girls I knew well on the cheek.

Billy said later: 'Those were the TV scouts.'

I knew they were, but I didn't care. I was pissed and just having a laugh. I didn't take it seriously. I guess I was just showing off.

But although I didn't know it, the scouts were having hurried discussions about me. It turned out that they'd been asking everyone who the biggest players were on the Newcastle scene and loads of people had said my name.

Even though I'd been out of it for nearly two years because of Emily, I was still legendary apparently.

MTV were planning a follow-up to the hugely popular American show *Jersey Shore*, and were testing different cities around the country for a British venue for the programme.

Everyone the scouts met who knew me had told them that if they were doing a Newcastle version, they had to have me in it. So when they'd run into me, they'd immediately put me to the test to see if I would live up to the hype.

Apparently I did, because before the night was over they'd found me again and asked for my number. 'Can we call you tomorrow?' Lauren asked. 'I'm actually from MTV.'

I agreed but didn't think I'd hear from them again. I expected they'd meet loads of people that night and the chances that I was exactly what they were looking for were slim.

The next day, I was hungover and helping Grandad out by being an escort on one of his minibuses. It was freezing cold and we were on the icy roads with a bus-load of loud people in the back.

When my phone rang I could hardly hear the girl on the other end until she said: 'It's Lauren from MTV.'

The events of the night before came back to me all at once and I was suddenly alert. 'Hi Lauren,' I said as calmly as I could. 'What can I do for you?'

'I wondered if I could give you a quick interview over the phone? It won't take long.'

I tried to block out the noise, and said that it was fine.

'What are you like with girls and how often do you go out?' she asked.

'I go out four or five times a week,' I replied. 'I've worked in Malia and banged 43 birds that summer.'

'What's your best story?'

'I've had a threesome with identical twins – does that count?'

'Okay–' she said, before I cut her off.

'I've banged everyone in Newcastle,' I went on, getting into the swing of things. 'I've had 200 birds and...'

On and on I went, telling her about all my nightly misdeeds and detailing some of my best shags. The more I told her, the more excited she got. Eventually she said she wanted me to do a face-to-face interview in Newcastle – in front of a television camera.

'It's for a new show we're planning called *Geordie Shore*,' she said. 'We think you'd be good on it.'

I said I'd heard of *Jersey Shore* but I'd never seen it. I'd watched a few episodes of *The Hills*, but I wasn't a big TV watcher, so I didn't really have a clue what she was on about. But I was never one to turn down an opportunity, so I agreed.

She said she'd send me a few DVDs so I could see what she was on about, and we arranged to meet in Newcastle for the interview.

It all seemed a bit unreal, and I doubted anything would come of it. But I wanted to give it my best shot, so that afternoon I went to see a mate of mine who had some experience in front of the cameras – Anthony Hutton.

He'd been on *Big Brother* so I reckoned he could tell me a bit more about what to expect.

'What's it all about?' I asked, after explaining that it was going to be based on *Jersey Shore*. 'Do you reckon I'd be good enough?'

'It's a TV show Gaz,' he said bluntly. 'Just fucking do it.'

'Really?'

'It's a simple show, man – you have a good time and pull birds. That's it. Are you kidding me? Do it!'

I began to get excited.

For the next two weeks, me and Billy did our Sky training and fantasised about what it would be like if I got on TV.

During that time I had my first face-to-face interview with Lauren and, as soon as they turned the huge cameras on and started rolling, I started sweating my tits off.

But once I got going, I forgot about the camera and got on with answering her questions, which were all about my sex life and nights out.

Then they arranged for me to go to London and meet the MTV execs at their base in Camden Town.

The whole thing was such a bizarre experience.

For the next few weeks I was shuttled back and forth between Newcastle and London, doing endless interviews with MTV – while training for the Sky job too. It was crazy.

I started work on the sales floor at Sky, and I instantly hated it. I was back in an office and had always hoped that my life would be different to that. I just wasn't an office person. Some people love sales, and make a lot of money doing it. Some people love working in an office – the camaraderie and the set working days suits them perfectly.

It just wasn't for me. But this TV thing was probably a nonstarter, and I needed it to fall back on, so I gave it a go.

Another girl I knew, Vicky, was working at Sky too.

I knew her from the Newcastle clubbing scene, and she was

a good lass. She'd dated one of my mates a few years back, and I'd never shagged her.

She was hot but, because she'd been a mate's girlfriend, she was off-limits. It was good to see a friendly face, though she was acting a bit weird, and I had my suspicions as to why...

She inexplicably quit soon after I started. She was actually the lass who was training me up and one minute she was there, the next she was gone. As I said, I was pretty sure I knew why. Because I must have been acting a bit weird too.

The TV people had told me not to tell anyone about the show, so I had to keep my mouth shut and it was so hard. I was going through the most exciting time of my life and I only had Billy to confide in. It was torture.

Amazingly I got through the TV screening process and found myself at the final interview, which they'd agreed to do in Newcastle. I needed time off work for it, so I had to come clean to my new boss. 'I'm sorry,' I said, 'but I've got to go to this thing at 2pm – it's for a TV show I might be on.'

He was absolutely sound about it all and told me to just go.

A few hours later, I was back at my desk, which backed onto Billy's. I stared at my computer screen and sighed loudly.

'This is shit, isn't it?' I told him. 'I'm off.'

Then I got up and walked out. I could feel Billy staring at me in shock as I left the floor.

I waited to him to finish work and caught him on the way out. He looked at me, dressed in his little shirt and tie, as if I was mad. 'What are you doing, you nutter?' he asked. 'You'll get sacked!'

'I won't be here next week, you're right,' I said, nodding my head.

'Seriously,' he said. 'What are you doing? Are you okay?'

'What am I doing?' I said. 'I'm going on fucking *Geordie Shore*, that's what I'm doing!'

I'd got in. I was the newest cast member of the newest TV series in the country. I had no idea what to expect, all I knew was that I'd be moving into a house with a group of other people in less than two weeks. And I still wasn't able to tell anyone about it.

It was so surreal. I'd actually signed the contracts that day and I was buzzing. They had given me my last interview, and then told me I was in and to get ready. I packed in my job, and went out on the lash with Billy to secretly celebrate.

The next day I told Mam, Grandad and Claire and I watched an episode of *Jersey Shore* with Mam. 'What do you think?' I asked her.

'The girls are a bit vile, but the lads are doing just what lads do,' she said.

'What would you think if I was one of them?' I asked.

'I guess they're just normal lads,' she admitted. I took that as a green light.

At that point, the show was going to offer me free food, free accommodation and free nights out. Plus it would be one heck of an experience. It sounded like a good deal to me.

I didn't expect it to last beyond the first series; I just assumed it was a one-off and thought it would be cool if anyone recognised me at all once it aired, but I doubted even that would happen.

'How mad would it be if people came up to you in the street,' Billy said, laughing.

'Nah,' I answered. 'That won't happen. Only us Geordie lot will bother watching it. I'm hardly gonna be famous.'

There was one more person I had to tell – my girlfriend,

Carly. I'd not told her anything so far, but I knew she needed to know what I was up to. I couldn't just disappear for a month without telling her.

And I also knew I couldn't go in the house if I had a girlfriend. We had to finish, even if it was only temporarily, and I hoped she'd understand. We'd only been together a few months and it wasn't that serious. Not like it had been with Emily.

If I'd been with Emily I would have turned it down. But although I cared about Carly, I knew this was a once-in-a-lifetime opportunity and that was exactly what I told her.

She didn't agree. And she begged me not to do it.

'You'll be famous,' she sobbed. 'I'll lose you.'

She'd had some experience of the fame game herself.

She was a singer with a great voice who had got through to the 'Judges' Houses' round on *The X Factor*, before being dropped in favour of the band JLS.

She had got so close to realising her dream of stardom but had fallen at the last hurdle. Now I felt that she was taking out her frustrations on me, because I was going on TV, where she'd always wanted to be.

She told me I was being selfish and we rowed for days – having the same argument over and over. It was exhausting. I was going to the gym every day, and trying to prepare myself for moving into the *Geordie Shore* house, and with all the stress I was under she was making me question my decision.

I just wanted her to be supportive. If it had been the other way round I would have given her a hug and wished her luck. She was basically telling me that if I did it I was a horrible human being.

GAZ (AND MY PARSNIP)

It was a tough time.

'I'm sorry,' I told her. 'I have to give this a go. I might make a fool of myself, I might be shit – I have no idea what will happen next. But I can't turn down this once-in-a-lifetime opportunity.'

'You're selfish,' she said. 'What about me?'

'You think I'm being selfish?' I said, getting angry. 'This is MTV! A chance at a future in telly.'

But she was so distraught I almost packed the whole thing in. Maybe I was being selfish. Maybe I was ignoring her feelings because it was something I wanted to do. I did care about her, after all. And I hated seeing her so upset. I was torn. Racked with indecision, I called Anthony for advice.

'Man this is killing me,' I said. 'I don't know what to do.'

'Gaz,' he said sternly. 'Man the fuck up. Stop snivelling, you're going in that fucking house.'

So I did.

PARSNIP POINTERS

NO. 10: THE WINGMAN/WINGWOMAN

Two is a good number. Three is even better. If you go out alone you're only going to look like a creepy loner. Girls steer well clear of creepy loners. But a guy who is laughing and joking with his mates? He's definitely a better prospect.

This is why you need a wingman or two. If you only have one wingman, and he doesn't pull, you'll be distracted by his loneliness. But two guys can back you up and keep each other company once you're working your magic on a lass.

You can also use a wingwoman: having hot female friends makes you look appealing to girls in general. Plus if they can see that girls are mates with you, they'll think you must have a sensitive side.

If your wingwoman is exceptionally hot, you might think this could be intimidating – but not if you explain that she's a pal. The fact that you've got such a hot mate and you can still restrain yourself around her reflects well on you. Bonus points.

CHAPTER 11

GEORDIE
SHORE

The final few days before I moved into the *Geordie Shore* house in Jesmond were surreal. A camera crew turned up to film me packing and I felt like I was under a microscope all the time.

But I knew I had to get used to it – I wouldn't have a moment to myself for the next six weeks. If I got spooked by some cameramen watching me pack for a few hours, I wouldn't last one night in the house that was to be my temporary home for over a month.

Finally, I said my goodbyes to Mam and Claire, and got driven to the house. I had to leave my mobile phone behind and we wouldn't have a telly or access to newspapers. All us housemates would have was each other.

We were being sent into the house one by one and I had no idea if I would be first, last or somewhere in between. The crew wished me luck, I took a deep breath and then opened the front door.

GAZ (AND MY PARSNIP)

It was quite quiet in the house, but I could hear chatting coming from one of the rooms, so I headed towards the noise.

The first person I saw was Vicky Pattison, and I wasn't surprised. I already knew her – she was the girl who had trained me at Sky, a girl I'd known for years, and I'd already had my suspicions she'd be in there. We grinned at each other, and said something sarcastic like, 'What a surprise!'

She was all dolled up and looked amazing, but that's just Vicky. She always looks stunning. She's a good lass and I was glad to see a friendly face.

After saying hi to Vicky I heard someone coming up behind me and turned to face a mountain of a man: Jay Gardner.

His arms were fucking massive, his huge hands were clutching a can of Red Bull – making it look like a toy – and his eyebrows were the most bizarrely perfect things I'd ever seen. I couldn't stop staring at him as he grabbed my hands for a shake. 'Oi, oi!' he said cheerfully, introducing himself. He reminded me of the lads I'd made friends with in college, and I knew instantly that we'd be mates.

I hardly even noticed Charlotte Crosby, the other girl who was sat on a sofa. She was so quiet, she didn't even register at first. I said hi, and she meekly told me her name, but it was obvious she was extremely nervous. I think she was a bit intimidated by Jay, who was pissed and swinging his arms around like a big gorilla. It seems funny now, looking back on it – they all seemed like completely different people from the group I now know so well.

Especially Charlotte – she would be such a huge part of my life on *Geordie Shore*, yet at first I didn't even notice her.

Having got myself a drink I started chatting, but it wasn't

long before we were joined by someone else: James Tindale.

I was so pleased to see him. I knew James really well, he'd been a mate for years. He was friends with Anthony Hutton and we'd often go and get smashed together. I used to do something called 'topless hosting' in Newcastle, and James used to sell the shots in the clubs to get people hammered. If the lads were going to be me, Jay and James then I knew the next six weeks would be a blast.

Next to arrive was Greg, and my first thoughts were: 'Who the fuck is this guy?'

Greg was a nice bloke, but he was completely different to the rest of us, and I could tell that straight away. He was older than us, a lot quieter, and a bit posh too. He was only a social drinker really – he liked to have a drink with a meal and then stop after a few. I remember pouring him a drink and all he kept saying was, 'What, another?'

He was very different to the rest of the crowd gathered in that room and stuck out like a sore thumb, nursing his drink for ages.

We were all getting a bit merry when the front door opened again and this whirlwind of a girl in a black tutu bounced into the room. It was Sophie Kasaei.

She looked a right state, bless her, and she was acting like some kind of gangster, shouting, 'Blak, blak, big up ya'self – where's the booze!'

Sophie was mad, and I remember thinking, 'Oh no, this is going to be a nightmare. Who the hell is this?'

I kept saying, 'What on earth are ya doing?' But she just giggled at me.

However I could see she was quite sweet really, and she was just trying to make a big impression. But Vicky – 'Queen

Vicky' – looked stunned. Her and Charlotte got pissed almost instantly, and were the first in the hot tub, fully clothed, rolling around and getting to know each other.

Me and Jay explored the house and instantly found the shag pad – a room cut off from the rest of the bedrooms, with low lighting and a huge bed.

I knew I'd be making use of that little room…

It wasn't long before me, Jay and James stripped off our tops and prepared for our own hot-tub action. I did a few press-ups and James worked on his arms – we wanted our first pec show to be as good as it could be. Greg stayed downstairs with Vicky, who'd moved into the kitchen, and it looked like they were getting very cosy.

Then Holly Hagan arrived.

Well, Holly's tits came in first and Holly followed soon after… Her ta tas were massive and everyone was pissed, so they didn't hold back from staring at them. She was dressed like some kind of demented goth fairy: studded gloves, huge hair and caked in make-up.

We've all changed so hugely since that first season, it's very strange to think back to that first night. It's like we were all different people compared with how we are today. I think we've grown so much now that we're not the same people as we were at that initial meeting.

None of us had a clue what we were doing, apart from maybe Holly, who had been a fan of *Jersey Shore*.

It was surreal. Was this the whole talent pool of girls I had to choose from? Vicky I knew already, Sophie was mad, Holly was a walking pair of tits and Charlotte I hadn't even noticed. It was nuts.

They're like family now and I love them all to pieces. But

back then, everyone had their game faces on and I had no idea what the next few weeks would bring.

Predictably, everyone got slaughtered and ran around the house like five-year-olds at a kids' party. Drunk five-year-olds. Wearing very little clothing. It was carnage.

Sophie was crawling around the floor with a wet patch down her pants from pissing herself, Charlotte was violently throwing up in the toilet, Vicky and Jay had disappeared together and Holly was letting her bazookas have some fresh air by taking her top off in the hot tub.

To be fair they were threatening to come out of their own accord anyway, so it didn't make much difference. I'm not actually a boob man, I go for bums more myself. So it didn't bother me that they were out, and it didn't bother me that they were massive. They could have been any size, I wasn't fussed.

But it was definitely a shock when a few hours later she boldly announced to everyone that she had a boyfriend.

We all thought the guy must have been mad to let her come on the show, knowing full well what she would get up to. 'She's probably going to bang all of us,' said James. 'He's mad.'

By this time she was drinking directly from a wine bottle and was slurring her words. We were all puzzled about what kind of guy her boyfriend was, whether he was okay with her being on telly flirting like she was.

'I can do what I want,' she said, as the lads poured booze over her tits. It was like being in some kind of porno film.

Holly said he would be fine if she messed around with any of the lads, as long as she didn't shag them. Everyone was shocked and wanted to hear all about it. But the more we questioned her, the more upset she got. She thought we were having a go at her, when actually we were just amazed and wanted to know more. Eventually she ran off crying and Vicky went to comfort her.

When everyone finally sloped off to bed Holly was still upset so I said she could share my bed. I know, I'm such a gentleman... But seriously I knew if she got in next to me it would be game on, and it was.

We had a bit of a kiss, but we didn't shag.

The next day we lazed around, getting to know each other and getting used to our new home. Then that night we had our first job – topless butlering on a party limo.

We always have a job to do every season, whether it's massaging, butlering, spray tanning... I wouldn't say anyone takes it very seriously, even though we're obviously supposed to. But I like a challenge, and back then everything was new to us, so at first I was willing to give it my all.

I could hear the girls screaming when they saw their outfits for the first time – tiny hot pants and boob tubes. Charlotte thought they were ace, but everyone else was a little apprehensive.

The lads thought what we had to wear was hilarious – little dickiebows and shorts. We were all ripped, so we weren't bothered about showing off our bodies. It would just be a laugh.

We sprayed each other with Veet, to make sure we were nice and smooth. No one likes chest stubble. Then we went downstairs and waited for the girls.

When they walked in I couldn't take my eyes off Charlotte. She looked amazing. Long legs, cute little bum, high heels – I couldn't believe I hadn't noticed how pretty she was before.

Above left: Need proof that the camera has always loved me? Check out my posing skills!

Above right: I'm trying out some early dance moves on my sister, Claire. I was obviously born to be famous.

Below: 'Outta my way!' Collecting another gold medal on my school Sport's Day.

Above: One of the many kiddy football teams I was part of as a lad. For most of my life I truly thought I would go pro.

Right: Here I am in Spain, lifting the winner's cup for my football team, Grainger Park. It was one of the best days of my young life.

Spanish magic for Tynedale youngsters

TWO boys from the district have helped their football team enjoy victory in a major international junior tournament in Barcelona – beating an Italian academy side in the final.

Gary Beadle, of Ruskin Court, Prudhoe, even scored in the 3-0 final win.

The seven-a-side under 11s "Trofeo Meditterrano Classic" tournament saw 16 teams from all over Europe compete in four groups, the winners of which went into two semi finals.

Newcastle club Grainger Park took two teams, one featuring Gary and the other featuring Tom Priestley, from Hexham.

Both sides won their respective groups but were unfortunate to meet in the semi final, where Gary's team went through although

only on penalties after a 1-1 draw.

Tom's team then went on to hammer a French outfit 9-0 in the third place play-off, while Gary's team secured the trophy.

The only English squad to take part, they collected the cup in a special presentation afterwards.

Parent Shirley Beadle, who went on the trip with a number of parents, said: "It was an amazing experience not just for the players but also for the parents and children who were there to support them.

"Although it was only European teams taking part, to the kids it was like a mini-World Cup, especially when they won.

"We only took part for the experience of playing against foreign teams, and it was a bonus when we won and took third place as well."

For the cabinet: Gary Beadle (right) with the tournament trophy, while Tom Priestley holds his league-winning team's cup

Left: Being in the public eye isn't a new thing – my mug has always made the news.

Above: Here's me at 16 with my proud mam, Shirley – just one day before leaving home to join the marines.

Below: 'The name's Beadle… Gary Beadle.' Making an effort for my first ever prom.

Above: Who needs the sun to go topless? We're proper Geordies! © *WireImage*

Below: Creating our kebab scented perfume – as you can see, we took the process very seriously! © *PA Images*

Above: 'Protect your Parsnip, lads!' One of my proudest moments: my very own range of condoms is launched.
© *Rex Features/Simon Ford*

Below: Suited and booted for MTV's EMA Awards, in 2012.
© *WireImage*

Above: Me and Scott weighing up our options with Tanya Tate at the 2013
Erotica Show in London.
© *Rex Features/Simon Ford*

Below: Pinned to the bed by a bunny girl? Well, you know what they say: all
work and no play...
© *Rex Features/London News Pictures*

Left: Out on the town with Vicky – we knew each other way before Geordie Shore started. © *FilmMagic*

Below: Here we are, promoting the Cancun series with our own beach at London's Liverpool Street Station. Sometimes I can't believe how my life has turned out.
© *PA Images/Matt Crosick/ Empics Entertainment*

Top: Preparing for a talk at the Oxford Union. They loved us!

© *Rex Features/ Greg Blatchford*

Below left: Me and our Charlotte. Whatever happens, we'll always be good mates.

© *WireImage*

Below right: With Charlotte, showing off the best legs in Newcastle. She'll always be a worldie to me!

© *WireImage*

She was in high spirits too, a lot more excited about the whole thing than the others. I loved her spirit. I just thought, 'Wow...' Quickly followed by, 'I'm going to bang her.'

We all got into the limo that had arrived to take us to work. All apart from Greg, who apparently was homesick and wanted to stay behind.

Vicky said Greg was feeling like an outcast and had been upset all day. I felt sorry for the lad – he was one fish who was seriously out of water. But it was our first night out and I couldn't believe he wouldn't even give it a chance.

Our 'boss', Anna, explained that we had to get people on board the limo and then keep them entertained. The lads were a man down so we had to work really hard to make a good impression for her.

But after a while I realised *Geordie Shore* wasn't about working. It was about entertaining the viewers at home, not the people in the party limo. There was a shag pad with my name on it, and I wanted to christen it.

Vicky, Charlotte, Sophie and Holly got stuck into the task at hand, coaxing loads of men onto the limo and handing them Ferrero Rocher chocolates.

Jay was snogging lasses to get them to go on the bus, and we were all flirting our arses off. It was no different to a normal night out really. But I kept staring at Charlotte. She looked amazing.

At one point she accidentally threw a glass of white wine over me and I looked down, going, 'What the fuck?'

But then she looked at me seductively and started rubbing it into my bare chest. All I could think was: 'You're going to get it...'

We kept mucking about, getting drunker as the night wore

on and I felt really horny for her. Her legs... Man, I couldn't believe I hadn't noticed them before.

To be fair, she felt the same way.

She'd not taken any notice of me when we'd met the day before. But for both of us, something definitely kicked off that night. On the way home, we snogged in the taxi and I told her I wanted her.

I tried to get her into bed, but she wouldn't shag me that night. She was determined to keep me waiting, and the more I waited the more I wanted her.

Waking up in the house was a weird experience for everyone. For a brief moment you'd forget where you were, but having a cameraman in your face while you rubbed your bleary eyes was a pretty instant reminder.

But even though we were aware of the cameras, they were easy to ignore after a while.

We settled into our real personalities and became much more natural with each other. It was an insane experience. We all made the absolute most of it, because we thought it was a one-off. There was no agenda. We just got drunk and pulled. Every night.

Nobody told us what to do. We just did what any bunch of Geordies would do if everything was paid for by someone else, and they had no real day jobs to occupy their time.

Yes we did have a token job for each season, but there was no real pressure and we knew it. And they were all 'party' jobs – it was more like being out on the town really. Except that we were treated like celebrities everywhere we went.

Every bar or club we went to, no matter how long the queue, we walked straight in. I remember seeing lads I knew in the queue and waving at them as I swept past. It was unreal.

We were always quickly ushered into the VIP areas and told to have a good time. And man, we did. The girls would chant 'Jager, Jager, Jager' and we'd throw back round after round of the stuff before getting onto the dance floor.

We had all day every day to deal with our hangovers, so we didn't hold back on nights out. It was mint. That first season, we basically just all got to know each other.

And I got to know Charlotte particularly well.

A couple of nights in, we were out again, and I made a beeline for her. She was hilarious and I was pretty transfixed by her. I realised that I wanted her so badly. Her and those legs. She was banging.

I was in there like swimwear – all over her.

I told her I'd not bother trying to pull anyone else if she agreed to go home with me, but she kept changing her mind: she was hot one minute, cold the next. Meanwhile, I could see Greg – Greg of all people – stuffing napkins with girls' numbers scribbled on them into his pocket and I started to feel that familiar competitive urge.

Eventually I turned away from Charlotte and gave my attention to the hundreds of other lasses in the club.

After a stunning effort on my part, I brought two girls back to the house that night. Charlotte was still being coy, and although I wanted to bang her, I wasn't going to spend the whole time mooning over her and not getting laid. I wanted to get on with it.

I took them to the shag pad, and asked Jay to join us. 'We can share,' I told him. 'Get involved.'

But he said no, so I had to shag them both. What a chore… Everyone thinks the first threesome in *Geordie Shore* happened in Series Three, but it actually happened back then in Series One. I was the first to shag in the house, and I did it with two birds at once.

It was pretty impressive. But for some reason no one really noticed. The cameras showed me going upstairs with two birds, and that was it. I guess it was pretty obvious what was going to happen next.

Eventually, a week or so in, I got Charlotte to come home with me after a night out. She was drunk and bigging herself up in the cab on the way back.

'You just want to shag us,' she said. 'But I wanna break your heart.'

I almost rolled my eyes.

'Yeah yeah,' I said. 'We'll see.'

'Who's gonna win?' she said.

I laughed. 'That's a cracking bet to be fair like.'

I knew she wouldn't break my heart – I'm too much of a player for that. But I had no idea it would eventually end up being the other way round.

We played a cat-and-mouse game for ages. I'd pull other birds and bring them back and she'd pretend she didn't care. Then I'd end up in bed with her and we'd mess around but she wouldn't let me shag her. It was an epic chase.

I'd tell her: 'I will shag you, you know.'

And she'd say: 'You won't.'

I'd just grin. 'I will, you just watch.'

Being in the house was mostly fun, but in that first season we didn't really have anything to do in the daytime, so we did get a bit bored.

We made up our own games, like MC-ing to the hoover. Sophie was a pro at that. And the girls loved messing around with make-up. Holly used to wear something ridiculous like nine pairs of false eyelashes at the same time, and we'd all just watch her carefully put them on until she looked like she had two tarantulas on her face.

'Holly,' we'd plead with her. 'Just wear one set. You don't need all those things on your face.'

But she was adamant she could do what she wanted. She was like the little sister of the house – we all looked after her, even if she annoyed us sometimes.

One Sunday, when the cameramen were off, and for some reason all the other lads were out too, it was just me and the girls in the house. Holly came over with her make-up bag and somehow convinced me to let her do me over. I ended up with eyeshadow and mascara all over me, and the girls were wetting themselves laughing.

Apparently I make a very attractive lady.

Our fridges were always stocked up with food but we weren't very good at cooking. The lads could do your bog standard meat-and-two-veg but that soon got boring.

Sophie, however, very quickly became the mum of the house. She was the one you'd go to if you wanted a friendly ear, and she was the one who cooked us all nice meals to eat together. She was no Gordon Ramsey, but she knew far more about cooking than the rest of us.

She made us cottage pie, lasagna, and a full Sunday roast at the weekends. She was a legend.

The lads were great and I spent most of my time in that first season with them.

We'd go out and pull together, and told each other stories about what players we were. Me and Jay were the complete opposite of each other but we got on so well. We constantly teased each other. When we were getting ready to go out he'd look me up and down and say: 'What the fuck is that T-shirt all about?'

And I'd stare back and say: 'Look at your own wardrobe, son – what the fuck is any of it all about?'

James would talk to everyone, he was just a decent, friendly guy. He had no issues and just wanted the world to have a good time. He even got on with Greg, which was a mystery to me.

I never 'got' Greg. He just wasn't really my cup of tea. I guess we didn't have all that much in common, but I thought he was a bit boring actually. He never wanted to come out and had nothing to say.

He was pretty miserable in the house to be honest and I didn't really spend much time with him. Maybe I sound a bit harsh, but I guess what I mean to say is that he was just very different to me. He was quiet, a bit posh, and I always got the impression he was trying to be something he wasn't.

We all showed off a bit in the beginning but we were all being ourselves really – mad, fun-hungry, sex-crazed drinkers. Deep down, Greg wasn't like that at all and as a result he just didn't fit in.

On the other hand, me and Charlotte got closer and closer as the days passed.

If I needed time away from the lads we'd disappear off together to the shag pad across the garden, and talk for hours, mostly about absolutely nothing.

We told each other about our lives, cuddled and napped together. I still tried to shag her, but she held off for weeks and I didn't really mind.

She was funny, caring and mega fit. I cared about her a lot

and I enjoyed being with her, even if we weren't doing anything other than chatting.

Besides – I knew I'd get her in the end. There was too much tension between us for it just to disappear without us banging.

Finally, as I predicted, we were in bed one night messing around when I decided to make my move. She was on top, playing with me and I just started edging the parsnip closer and closer to the promised land. We finally shagged.

Afterwards she jokingly told me off, but she wanted it as badly as I did. After that we banged regularly, even though I pulled other girls too.

I was honest with her and told her we weren't going to be together as a couple. At first I thought she felt the same way, but I was obviously very wrong, because we kept arguing about it. And she did eventually admit she had feelings for me.

But I was clear – we were just having fun. I didn't want anything else from her. Sometimes it was like she accepted it, other times she got upset.

It got very tough sometimes.

Vicky and Jay were having the same sort of problems as me and Charlotte and the tension in the house grew unbearable at times. Greg and Holly fell out, Vicky fell out with the girls, Jay and Vicky were kissing one minute and screaming at each other the next – it was exhausting.

The problem was, we couldn't get away from each other. In the real world, when people argue they can go and let off steam and have some time to themselves. We couldn't. We had to face our issues immediately, and it was difficult.

People might watch the show and wonder how things could escalate to such epic fights, and the only thing I can say is this: you try living with people you don't know, unable to really escape to clear your head. You'll soon understand why we exploded every now and again.

And it really was only every now and again to be honest.

We're in the house for a long time each season and our viewers only see an hour of every week that passes.

Everyone always sorted their problems out eventually, and we got really close. It was like being a big family – yelling at each other one minute, laughing with each other the next.

All of us could see Charlotte was getting genuinely upset at the situation that was developing between us, but no one had a go at me – at least not in the beginning. They could see she kept coming back for more, even though she knew the score. I didn't want to hurt her, but when she crawled into my bed I wasn't going to say no, was I?

Sophie was great at keeping the peace. She'd listen to both sides of the story, and comfort Charlotte without taking sides. We began calling ourselves the tripod. We three stuck together, because if one leg fell, we'd all fall.

We quickly got used to all the free food and lounging around and I can honestly say, looking back, it was my favourite season of all. We've done so much more since then, had so many more adventures – but that first month was such an exciting time. We had no idea what would happen afterwards, and we just let rip.

Everyone was just shagging and drinking, arguing and making up. It was like some kind of mass orgy.

There was one night when Sophie was shagging some lad and she whispered 'chlamydia' in his ear – fuck knows why.

When we heard we fell about laughing. Why would you say that to someone, mid-sex? She couldn't remember.

There was another night when we were out working at this

rough little social club, and Jay disappeared. I looked for him everywhere but he wasn't inside, so I went out back to see if he'd pulled.

Sure enough, I found Jay outside with his trousers down by his ankles shagging a bird. I creased over laughing, especially since a cameraman had followed me out and ended up filming his little arse pounding away.

But there was a downside to all this undiluted pleasure. After a string of arguments between everyone had left tensions at a record high, Holly left the house for a while.

That was after Jay had called her a cunt, which made Vicky fall out with him too. Vicky may not have been Holly's biggest fan back then, but she thought yelling at her like that was out of order and told him so.

Eventually Holly returned, but people were still not getting on with her. We swapped our bedrooms around to accommodate everyone's various dramas, and I ended up bunking in with Charlotte.

On the final night, we all went out and got steaming drunk as usual. Charlotte got so pissed in such a short time that Sophie had to take her home early.

A few hours later, I brought a girl back, and for some reason I ended up shagging her on the bed next to where Charlotte was lying, having passed out. I had promised Charlotte I would never have sex with someone else in front of her, and even now I'm not entirely clear how it happened. I think all the other beds were full.

I thought she'd sleep through it – she had been so drunk I was convinced she was out for the count. But she did wake up and she was devastated when she saw what I was doing, right next to her.

GAZ (AND MY PARSNIP)

It was a shitty thing to do, I admit. Especially when she stormed out crying and sat on the stairs sobbing. I knew she was upset but I just carried on banging the girl anyway. I was drunk and mid-shag. I wasn't going to stop.

The next day I tried to apologise to Charlotte, but she was still upset. I didn't know what else to do. I cared about her, but I didn't think I could commit to her. We were on the show to shag around and have fun. Starting a relationship would hardly make good TV.

Like all good things, though, *Geordie Shore* eventually had to come to an end. Despite all our little tiffs, everyone was sad to say goodbye when we had to leave the house.

We all got emotional, and there were definitely a few tears as we all packed our bags and promised to stay in touch. I really didn't want to leave. The whole thing had been heaven to me. Partying and drinking with a great group of mates for free – why the hell would I want it to end?

But, with our exciting six weeks over, we all had to move on. I walked out of the house in Jesmond and went back to my normal life.

PARSNIP POINTERS

NO. 11: DEALING WITH AN ENEMY ATTACK
Never mow another man's lawn. If a lass you're eyeing up in a club is there with another lad, even if she seems to be flirting with you, let her make the first move.

Don't move in while he's off in the toilets or at the bar, as this can end in disaster of the fisticuffs variety. Respect your foes.

Even if she makes her way over to you, you've got to be really careful how you play it. If a guy's got a flirty girlfriend, it's his problem – don't let him work it out with your face.

If it looks to be too much hassle, move on.

If another man breaks the rules and starts putting the move on the girl you're working on, don't worry. Act as if you're not even remotely threatened by him and let your wing buddies distract him. They should be ready to spring into action on just such an occasion – they can start chatting to him to keep him clear of you and your bird.

Alternatively, if you can see she finds him annoying, look her in the eyes and say you'll be right back.

This shows you're confident she's yours and gives her the time to be really hacked off by the other guy while also eagerly anticipating your return.

She'll want you to come back, and wanting you is exactly what you're angling for. Plus, you get the chance to save her – like a proper knight in shining armour.

Come back pretty sharpish with two glasses of champagne – one for you and one for her. He'll soon get the message.

CHAPTER 12

BACK TO REALITY

After our first stint on the show was over, I went straight back to my old life, convinced that nothing would change. I moved back in with Grandad and caught up with my family and friends.

Jay did the same thing and we chatted a few days later. We both discussed how weird it was to be back home, without everyone.

After the loudness of the girls in the house, everything seemed so quiet in comparison. Now all we could do was wait for the first series to come out, so we could laugh at ourselves and our antics.

We all kept in touch and were looking forward to seeing ourselves on telly. But the first air date was months away and I didn't have a clue what to do in the meantime.

Those next few weeks were surreal. One minute I had been with people every second of the day, eating and drinking as much as I wanted, my every move captured by cameras. Now I was sat on my arse on my grandad's sofa again. Alone. It felt pretty weird.

However, MTV soon got in touch to tell us we had to go through media training to prepare for any interviews we might have to do, and so in the end I was kept pretty busy.

We met all the important MTV people, and were helped with setting up our individual Twitter accounts. I'd never had one before, and had no idea how to do it, but all my friends had told me I really should get into social networking. I looked at various famous celebrities' accounts and couldn't believe how many people were following them. I was a nobody, why would anyone want to follow me?

In the weeks that followed, my phone buzzed regularly with calls and texts from MTV. In the run-up to the launch of *Geordie Shore* a lot of newspapers and magazines were apparently interested in who the cast of the show were.

Suddenly there were photo shoots and interviews, news-papers and magazines wanted to know all about us – and we couldn't really understand it. We weren't on the telly yet – why did they care?

But we went along with it, wearing what they wanted us to wear and posing in the way they wanted us to pose. It was fun. We felt like we were playing at being famous.

On the night the very first episode aired – 24 May 2011 – we were given a private screening an hour before the rest of the country was due to see it. MTV hired out a big room in a casino in Newcastle and laid on a party for us all. We were allowed to invite five guests (family and friends) each. I didn't take Mam because I didn't know what she would think and I wanted to vet it all first. Instead I took Billy and Anthony

Hutton and a few other lads. We had a couple of drinks and finally the screening began.

We had no idea how telly worked – we didn't have a clue about editing, music or camera angles. So when it began we were absolutely amazed. It was mental. We genuinely thought it was fucking hilarious to see ourselves shagging and falling around drunk. It was a good show. We could see that. And I certainly didn't object to Charlotte constantly describing my dick as a parsnip. But we didn't think it would make us stars, and I had no idea my 'parsnip' would go on to achieve such legendary status.

The series would be comprised of six one-hour episodes, broadcast once a week. So for the next six weeks I expected a few people might recognise me in Newcastle, and it would be a great pulling story for the future. Especially with all that talk about the size of my manhood... That was practically free advertising.

But after that, I was convinced my life would go back to normal.

I had no idea how wrong I was.

When I got back from the screening, Mam did not look impressed. 'We need to have a word,' she told me. 'What do you think you are doing? I didn't bring you up to behave like that.'

I couldn't help it, I just had to laugh. 'Mam,' I told her, 'I've been given a licence to party.'

'Yes,' she said, still looking serious. 'But it's madness.'

I tried to explain: 'I'm just doing what every other lad my age is doing,' I said. 'Except that you get to see it because I'm doing it in front of the cameras. It's a job. And I'm good at it.'

It took her a while to come around, but she understands

now and is proud of me. She knows that I've actually got my head screwed on and that I take it all as seriously as any other job I might have ended up doing as a career.

Of course I still have to work hard, like everyone else in the world. It just so happens that my job is to go out and have a good time.

That night, after the show had aired, my phone began to go crazy with Twitter notifications.

I couldn't read them fast enough – so many people were following me after watching the show. I had 5,000 followers in a matter of hours, and the number kept rising.

The next day I went down to the Metro Centre for a nose around the shops. As soon as I got there, I was mobbed.

'Gaz, Gaz, can I have a picture?'

'Gaz, sign this for my sister, she loves you...'

'Gaz, you're a legend!'

It was truly unreal.

But I didn't really have time for it to sink in, because just weeks later I had a phone call from MTV. Over half a million people had watched the first episode. And they had returned to watch the second and third episodes too. It was officially a hit show, and now they wanted to take us to Magaluf for a one-off Summer Special.

However, the even better news was that they had another offer for me: they wanted Charlotte and me to go to Australia to promote the show's forthcoming release there. It was due to air 'down under' in a few months' time and they wanted to drum up publicity for it. How could I say no? I packed my bags and got ready to party.

Arriving in the blazing Antipodean sunshine, me and Charlotte were like excited kids. I'd never been so far away from Newcastle in my entire life and couldn't believe I was the other side of the world from everyone and everything I'd ever known.

MTV had organised some big press events and parties to publicise the show and our schedules were so packed it would be a whirlwind tour.

We were invited on countless radio shows and magazine shoots and even found ourselves being interviewed on national TV talk shows. I remember sitting next to Audrina Patridge from *The Hills* in the green room on one show and feeling overwhelmed by it all.

I'd watched that programme when I was on the dole in Newcastle, and now I was sat next to its star, about to be interviewed on a level with her. I could hardly speak I was so nervous.

I went to some crazy parties while I was there, including one where I met a girl called Erin McNaught, a ridiculously hot Australian model and TV presenter.

She's now with the rapper Example, but back then she was single and seemed very interested in me. We had a few drinks and ended up getting on really well. The whole thing was surreal but I loved every second of it.

So many people wanted their pictures taken with me and Charlotte, I thought I was going to go blind from all the flashes.

How had I got here?

One minute I'd been on the dole, down to my last few quid, about to start a mind-numbingly boring job, which I knew wouldn't last. Now I was having sex with models and giving interviews about my life on TV shows that were watched by millions of people.

GAZ (AND MY PARSNIP)

When we got back, I only had a few days at home before I found myself re-packing my bags – this time to go to Magaluf. It was time to face the cameras again.

CHAPTER 13

MAGALUF MADNESS

The villa MTV had found us in Magaluf was like a palace, and from the first moment we walked through its doors we all knew we were going to have a mint time there. The weather was awesome, the beaches were perfect and I was on familiar territory: holiday pulling was my speciality, after all.

I didn't know how things were going to be with Charlotte, but I hoped she'd see that we had jobs to do. We were being put on telly to be filmed having a good time – we had to respect each other and get on with it.

Everything had been fine between us in Australia, where we'd been shepherded by professionals everywhere, and were kept busy with our never-ending promotional duties. But now we were back with the other housemates and would be left to our own devices. It could easily end up in disaster if we carried on with our little fling.

On the first night, we all arrived and explored our new

surroundings. But Vicky was nowhere to be seen. Apparently she was nervous about coming in because of all the arguments she'd had with Jay.

We didn't know whether she would come back at all, and so things felt a little strained.

While we were unpacking, Mark, who was our new 'boss', arrived and introduced himself. He told us that one person had to be in the villa at all times – it could never be left unattended.

We nodded and agreed to the new rules. But as soon as he left we all got ready and went out clubbing.

Sorry Mark.

I got into the swing of things instantly, and it wasn't long before I got up on stage to show off in front of the other clubbers. I was a teensy bit drunk, and decided to act out various sex positions in front of everyone – it's always good to advertise what you can offer.

And I could see Charlotte watching me as I bent over and displayed my best 'thrusting action' to the crowds. But she was being aloof, and said she was adamant that she wasn't bothered what I got up to. So I left her to it and cracked on with pulling the fittest birds around.

By now we were totally used to all the cameras. It was mad how quickly it became normal having them around, and we even made friends with the crew, who are a mint bunch.

We'd have a laugh with them in their downtime, and sometimes they got so distracted when they were laughing hard at our antics that they could hardly keep filming.

So we were like one big family. But as with all families, arguments were never far away.

At the club on that first night, Greg, Jay and I were asked to judge a wet T-shirt competition. 'Game on,' we thought. 'Let's see what the ladies have to offer.'

None of us were surprised when Holly decided to enter – we knew she was a show-off, especially where her boobs were concerned. But we were shocked when she started snogging a fellow contestant on stage. She really went for it, and I guess it changed certain people's views of her.

After all the arguments that had gone on in Jesmond, we didn't know how things would be in Magaluf. Holly had not really got on that well with the other girls in our first month together, and had sometimes been a bit of an outsider. She wasn't as much on the group's outskirts as Greg, who, unlike Holly, didn't often join in with anything; but she still hadn't been fully accepted by everyone.

I'd not had a problem with her – it was the girls, really. But tension between a group of girls can really poison an atmosphere, and we could all feel Holly was getting nowhere, no matter how hard she tried.

But that night she was a proper trooper and we all told her so.

We crowned her the winner and she was over the moon.

It was great to be back with everyone and we were all in high spirits – and full of other kinds of spirits – when we returned to what we thought would be the empty villa.

Jay had two random girls with him and immediately made his way to the shag pad to have his way with them.

But the villa wasn't empty.

Vicky had arrived while we were out getting trashed and, with all the beds taken, she'd decided to bed down in the shag pad.

So Jay was more than a little surprised when he found her

in the bed he was planning on shagging the girls in – especially with the tension that had been between them the last time we'd all been together. They'd had a short relationship and it hadn't ended well.

We all expected that after seeing him with two lasses, a huge argument would start between them. But Vicky was so calm, it was unnerving. She just got up and said she was happy to get out of the way.

We all went to bed. I had a hot blonde with me, so I didn't get much sleep. The parsnip did his business for a good few hours before I finally crashed out.

The next day I waved the lovely lass off as early as I could and we all went to the beach to relax – but before that, Mark turned up and had a go at us for breaking the rules on the very first evening.

As punishment, two people would have to stay in that night. I volunteered, and wasn't surprised when Greg decided to stay in too. He was always happier at home when we'd been in Jesmond and here in Magaluf, even with the sunshine and the new bars to explore, he obviously hadn't changed.

I wasn't exactly excited about the prospect of a night in with Greg, so I called a girl I'd met the night before and invited her round for a drink – and a shag. Score!

Being in Magaluf reminded me a lot of my time in Malia, but this was even better. Now, we were going out with strippers, drinking champagne and we had an amazing villa to take the lasses back to, rather than the dorm-like room I'd had in Malia. It was more than awesome.

On the night we partied with the strippers, the girls had said they were going to stay in and have a quiet one, so we felt like we'd just been let off our leashes. It was just us lads and a load of topless girls who were happy to grind away on our laps. We felt like millionaire rappers.

We came back relatively early – and without any playmates – after deciding to spend the rest of our night partying with our housemates at the villa. But it was empty and we quickly realised the girls had lied about staying in.

And so we had a few more drinks, ate takeaways and waited for the lasses to turn up. Eventually they came back – accompanied by a load of lads they'd pulled. We weren't happy.

All the girls had actually been a lot more cautious in Magaluf than they had been in Newcastle for the first series of *Geordie Shore*. They'd had quite a bit of Twitter abuse since it had begun to air, and had been cruelly accused of being slappers and slags.

It had actually upset them, and made them feel a bit down. It didn't seem fair, especially since they hadn't been nearly as bad as us lads, and we'd had nothing but praise for our own shagging antics.

While we were getting high-fived in the street, the girls had been putting up with a lot of nastiness. Sophie had actually decided not to shag anyone else whilst on the show, to save herself the trouble of any more aggravation.

So they'd all agreed to tone things down a bit, and this was the first bit of action they'd really had. They couldn't wait to get the six lads back and have a pool party.

But we were mad that they'd lied and gone out – Mark would be pissed off with us again, and rightly so, for leaving the house empty earlier in the evening.

When the girls walked in with all those strangers, screaming and shouting, us lads all retreated to the garden.

The girls thought we were jealous, and shouted at us about

our apparent double standards. But we weren't jealous at all – we were just pissed off that they'd lied and would obviously get us into more trouble with our boss. Their selfishness was maddening.

We went to bed and left them to it, but they were making so much noise in the pool we couldn't sleep.

I lost my rag a bit and went downstairs to yell at them to keep it down. Me and Charlotte ended up having a huge row in front of everyone, and for her it was obviously about more than simply just wanting to have a party. She was angry about how things were between us, and was clearly trying to make me jealous. It was so obvious it was almost embarrassing.

She got louder and louder and eventually screamed: 'Fuck off Gaz!'

So I ran upstairs and starting chucking her clothes around in anger. Eventually me and the lads went into the kitchen to cool down and it was then that the girls let rip at us. 'You bring girls back every night and we have to put up with it, and now we're not allowed?'

Charlotte was raging: 'Just go to fucking bed, Gary!'

'I can't,' I said, finally losing it completely, ''cause your loud ugly mouth is going on and on like that...'

I knew as soon as I said it I shouldn't have.

You should never call a girl ugly. Ever. Even if it's only in anger. Even if you don't mean it. They never forgive you. They may they say they do, but it will always come back to haunt you. And it hurts them really deeply, which is not good for either of you.

Vicky told me off and said that I'd gone too far. But she was just screeching in my face and all I wanted was for her to shut up.

144

Even now, with the benefit of hindsight, I honestly think that if they hadn't lied about staying in, the bust-up would never have happened. We were angry with them for a valid reason even if they couldn't see it.

When I'd had to stay in with Greg, I made the most of the situation. I kept my word and I didn't go out – for the good of the gang. Instead, they'd lied to us. They knew they were planning to go out and they sneakily told us they weren't.

But even so, I knew I shouldn't have said what I did.

Charlotte was obviously really upset with me. There was nothing I could do about it right at that moment though, so I sloped off back to bed and tried to ignore the huge amount of noise, which continued to come from downstairs until the early hours of the next morning.

The following day, the girls and the guys were still divided on the matter – none of us wanted to talk to any of them, and they were happy to comply.

We had a massive pool party to go to, which we'd all been really excited about. But that was before our meltdown. Now we were all seething with rage, and had to just hope that we could ignore each other enough to have a good time.

At lunchtime, a load of cars arrived to take us to the party. The last thing I wanted was to be anywhere near Charlotte, but I ended up in a cab with her – and with Vicky too.

They spent the whole time giggling about how much fun they'd had the night before and how great the lads were. It was pathetic. I concentrated on staring out of the window in silent protest, trying not to show them how angry I really was.

By the time we arrived, after that torturous car journey, I was fully ready to 'revenge pull'. Screw them all, I thought. I wasn't going to let them ruin my holiday with their pettiness.

I touched base with the other lads, and we all agreed we felt the same way.

It was time to go on a girl rampage...

Walking out to the pool area, we could see that there were lasses everywhere – it was a pulling paradise. Fake tits, big tits, small tits, tight bums, pert bums, plump bums – it was like walking into a shop that sells all your favourite sweets. Which ones do you try first?

I waded into the water and it wasn't long before I was lying in the shallow end with a topless brunette straddling me. With a little bit of strategic manoeuvring, we managed to shag in full view of everyone – without displaying the finer details of what we were doing. The lads were impressed, but Vicky just shouted: 'Nice one, Gary. Sure your mam's proud.'

A few nights later we all went out clubbing again, and as the night wore on I realised I didn't have a bird to take home. Panic began to set in. I kept spotting Charlotte and she was alone too. She was looking hot and before I could stop myself, I was cracking on to her. It was time to 'reopen the bank...'

'Do you wanna spoon tonight or not?' I asked her, getting straight to the point. Despite our recent rows, I was pretty confident she'd say yes, and when she didn't I was gobsmacked. I skulked off to lick my wounds and eventually went home alone. My bank account was apparently fully closed.

But back at the villa, I could see Charlotte was wavering. The banker was having second thoughts, and I took advantage of the opportunity this was giving me.

It wasn't long before we fell into bed together, giggling. She obviously couldn't resist the parsnip, and he was quite happy to have his wicked way with her.

Eventually, we managed to make up with the girls and the

rest of the holiday was a complete blast. On the last night we threw a huge pool party, and invited everyone we'd met in Magaluf back to the villa.

I cracked on and pulled a lass right away.

Then we went out clubbing to make the most of our last few hours in Magaluf. I was having a great time, dancing with the lads, chatting up a final girl to take home – when Charlotte suddenly decided she wanted to have a little heart-to-heart.

I was not impressed at the interruption, but we went and sat on a sofa and I let her rant on about how awful I was. I listened for about 10 seconds and then my mind just wandered. She had stuff to say, fine. But I didn't have to listen to it. Not on the last fucking night.

I'd only wanted to reopen the bank temporarily. But now me and Charlotte were back to square one and it was my own fault.

After a while she got up and walked off, sarcastically calling me a player before she went. 'Goodbye Gary,' she said, looking at me over her shoulder. My blood boiled.

When I got back downstairs, the girl I'd been chatting up had gone. Thanks Charlotte. But at least I'd had loads of sex on our holiday. James hadn't had one lass, the poor lad.

That night I had a lot to think about.

The arguments between me and Charlotte had been getting way out of control, which seemed stupid when we obviously both cared about each other. We were stuck in a game of one-upmanship and both of us were losing.

The next day, as we were packing to go home, I admitted I had developed feelings for her. I hoped it would help make things a little better between us. I was way off the mark.

PARSNIP POINTERS

NO. 13: USE PROPS

If you see a bunch of girls with a camera, go over and ask them if they want you to take a photo of them all. Take a couple of snaps, then turn the camera around and take a selfie before handing it back.

You're being kind, funny and a little bit cheeky – it's a great way to break the ice.

If the lass you've got your eye on is glued to her phone, go and ask her if you can borrow it. Call yourself before handing it back and saying you were too shy to ask for her number.

From here you can either strike up a conversation, or walk away and text her a bit later. A good one is to go to the bar, stand where you can see her and text to ask if she wants a drink. When she looks around to see where you are, you're standing there, cash in hand, ready to be served – and giving her a winning smile. Who can resist you?

CHAPTER 14

FAME AND FORTUNE

Back in Newcastle, my life became a whirlwind of activity. My Twitter followers were mounting up, I was being inundated with requests for interviews, and suddenly I was getting recognised everywhere I went. But I didn't see how I was going to make any money out of the whole thing, and I couldn't just go on the dole, poor but famous.

Luckily, MTV had other plans.

'You have to get an agent,' I was told at my next meeting with them. 'And quickly. They'll help you capitalise on your newfound fame.'

Since I didn't have a clue who would be good and who wouldn't, I just went with what everyone else was doing. I didn't care who it was – I was enjoying just being on the show, so if someone was going to help me make some money out of it too, then that was just a massive bonus.

My first meeting with my new agent was very informative.

'You've got five personal appearances to do this week,'

GAZ (AND MY PARSNIP)

I was told, before being given the relevant dates, times and locations.

In fact I wasn't sure exactly what it meant I'd be doing, and when they told me the details, my eyes nearly popped out of my head. 'You'll get paid this sort of fee go to a club and get pissed with their customers,' they explained, pushing a piece of paper towards me. On it was written a four-figure sum.

I would be getting paid just to go to a club? I couldn't believe it.

For the next month, while the show was being aired on MTV, me and the other *Geordie Shore* lads went on a PA tour, going all over the country getting paid to appear at clubs.

We had a driver to take us everywhere, and my bank account was soon showing figures I'd never imagined I'd see.

Things always got messy and it was ridiculous fun. We were apparently famous and got treated like royalty everywhere we went. We got pissed for free and the birds were practically throwing themselves at us. We got laid every single night, picking only the best girls to come back to our hotel and party with us privately.

I bought an iPad and started a chart of where we'd been and who I'd shagged. It was hilarious.

On top of getting paid thousands of pounds a week, mountains of free clothes and other stuff began turning up at Grandad's house.

Companies were falling over themselves to get me to wear their brands so people would see it on the show and want to buy it themselves. It was sheer madness, and slowly I began to see how the whole fame game worked.

If you were on telly, people loved you. The girls wanted to shag me and the lads wanted to 'be' me. For the clubs, it was a no-brainer to invite us to visit. They paid us to turn up, advertised that we were going to be there and people flocked to party with us – parting with a heap of cash at their premises while they were doing it.

I had no idea how long it would all last, but when I got asked if I wanted to film another series, I jumped at the chance. If this was to be my life for even just the next year I was going to make a fortune.

By now it was October 2011. I'd only been approached by MTV back in February, and the last eight months had been absolutely amazing. Free holidays, free accommodation, free clothes, money, hundreds of birds – I couldn't believe how much my life had changed.

I'd been coasting for years, with no clue what to do, scrabbling around for pennies just to get by. Now I was flush and famous.

I hoped it would last forever and I couldn't wait to get back together with the gang and begin filming Series Two.

Another round of shagging and boozing in Newcastle? I couldn't pack my things fast enough...

When I arrived at our new and improved *Geordie Shore* house – an amazing warehouse conversion on the outskirts of the city – I was buzzing.

Everyone was there apart from Greg, who'd decided to leave the show after we got back from Magaluf. I wasn't surprised. I guessed it just wasn't for him. We'd all seen he wasn't entirely comfortable with everything.

Charlotte looked as hot as ever, and I didn't waste any time in trying to get into her pants again. She was adamant she was going to stay away from me for good this time, but I reckoned there was still a little more credit left in the bank.

GAZ (AND MY PARSNIP)

When I first saw newcomer Ricci Guarnaccio, standing in the kitchen with a huge grin on his face, I couldn't help but laugh.

I knew the lad already; he was actually a good mate of mine. So I knew we'd have a blast now he was on board.

Vicky had recognised him right away too – she had seen him around and had always thought he was a good lad. Apparently they had hugged for quite a while when he first walked through the door, and it was quickly obvious that she fancied him. He liked her too, that was for sure. They instantly began flirting like teenagers.

We all had a few drinks and a catch-up, and Sophie and Vicky surprised us by announcing that they now had boyfriends outside of the house and were determined to be good girls.

I had no such plans to be well behaved.

I'd recently met a lass called Becca and she was a special girl, but we weren't an item. We were just close mates, and she totally understood what I would get up to when I wasn't with her.

We're still close, actually – even today. Whenever I'm not filming I regularly go over to her house for some rest and relaxation. She's a lovely girl and so easy to get on with.

Anyway, back then, I wasn't even sure that Sophie and Vicky would cope with their new plan – Sophie had sneaked a vibrator into the house to keep herself occupied, but who knew how long that would satisfy her for?

Everyone looked different somehow – a little more primped and preened, if that were possible. Sophie had dyed her hair blonde, and Holly now had loud red hair to match her loud personality.

We did a quick headcount: there were eight of us in the house so far. But there were nine beds and nine seats at the table, so I had a good idea that another person was on their way. Would it be a lass or a lad?

When the door finally opened, we all held our breath in anticipation. Rebecca Walker strutted in, all bubbly and energetic – a pretty brunette in a lovely red dress.

She was a good-looking lass. Nice arse, nice tits – the lads all approved. She obviously wanted to get stuck in right away, and walked over confidently to introduce herself to everyone.

Us lads all greeted her warmly, but the girls were much more reserved in their welcome. It was clear she'd have a lot of work to do to win them over. Especially Vicky, who was instantly stony-faced with the poor lass.

'She's got an attitude,' Vicky said, when she was a safe distance from the new girl. 'It's literally palpable.'

The others tried to include her a little bit, complimenting her on her outfit to break the ice. 'I had that dress,' said Sophie. 'It's nice.'

'I had it too,' said Vicky, smiling. 'But I took it back.'

Ouch.

The lads left them to it, and we gathered around for a few drinks in the kitchen. We didn't want to get involved in any nastiness, and had tried to make Rebecca feel welcome to compensate for the cold shoulder she was getting from Vicky.

Charlotte was getting a bit green-eyed too, and when I gave Rebecca a high-five after a bit of banter, she looked disgusted.

This was going to be a long night...

After a while, the girls shuffled off to one of the bedrooms for some kind of emergency meeting, leaving Rebecca with us.

We could clearly hear them slagging her off, saying things like she looked like Nancy Dell'Olio on crack.

I thought they were being ignorant and rude. It wasn't fair. I took Rebecca for a tour of the house, simply to get her away from them. I was determined to make her feel comfortable, and told her not to worry, that everyone would be fine with her in the end.

But when we got back to the main room, Rebecca and Vicky predictably began to argue. They were like hissing cats – neither of them would back down. It was soon obvious that Vicky, who had always been the house queen bee, had really met her match with fiery Rebecca. I thought it was funny, watching them tear strips off each other verbally.

Ricci had his own way of dealing with the situation – he just marched up to Vicky and snogged her. At first she tried to carry on the argument, but Ricci just planted his lips on hers whenever she tried to speak and eventually she calmed down.

And to top off our first night back, me and Charlotte ended up in bed together. Holly summed everything up neatly when she said: 'What the fuck? Welcome back to *Geordie Shore*...'

Despite ending up with Charlotte again, the following evening I was determined to go on the pull. Everyone was doing themselves up in preparation for a big boozy night, and I got ready while chatting to Rebecca.

'I'm gonna pull tonight,' I told her.

'What if that doesn't work?' she asked.

'I'll come back here and bang Charlotte,' I said, laughing.

She called me a prick. But I was only being honest.

We got stuck in at the club, and I pulled pretty quickly, which Charlotte wasn't too impressed about. It made her well jealous and she got absolutely blitzed. She could hardly stand up, so Ricci took her home to look after her, scoring major points with the girls. They all got goo-goo-eyed over him for that. It was a nice move.

Over the next few days we all had a right laugh together, going out every night and getting absolutely mortal. Rebecca even managed to make it up with Vicky, which was a relief. But Charlotte was still not happy with our relationship and wasn't afraid to let me know about it.

On one such night out, I was busy working my magic on a girl when Charlotte staggered over and interrupted me to have one of our 'chats'.

I was totally cockblocked – I couldn't leave to have a little natter with Charlotte and still shag the bird I was chatting up, and I couldn't shag Charlotte because she was too drunk.

It was a lose-lose situation.

It may have made good telly, but it was genuinely hard on us at times. We all cared about each other but we were always arguing about one thing or another. The fuck hut, located in our garden, saw a lot of action – and not all of it was of the shagging kind. We should have called it the drama room instead, because we were constantly fighting in there.

I knew that shagging other birds would get me into trouble, but I couldn't help myself. I was single. I wanted to sleep with as many girls as I could.

The lasses thought I was a total sleazeball, especially when one cheeky bird decided to give me a hand job in the hot tub one night – while everyone else was in it too.

Things got a bit heated between everyone. Ricci and Vicky got very close, making her feel guilty about her boyfriend on the outside. Jay and Rebecca were getting close too, though their budding fling was not without its problems.

GAZ (AND MY PARSNIP)

And Charlotte and I began to argue a lot. It got so bad that she even left the house for a while, which was a bit of a shock.

While she was gone, me and Jay went out alone to get wasted and pull a few worldies. It was wicked, although I eventually went home alone. Jay, however, brought a girl back and immediately took her to the fuck hut, leaving Rebecca with a face like a pissed-off pitbull.

She came to see me in bed for a chat. It was all perfectly innocent, but when Jay saw her in my room he thought I was trying it on with her. I wasn't – he was a mate and I knew he liked her, so she was off limits. But he didn't believe me, and we had a huge row.

We ended up pushing each other around a bit and it almost turned into a punch-up. Luckily, Sophie intervened in the nick of time and managed to defuse the situation.

I was upset. I didn't want to lose Jay as a mate and I couldn't understand how he could think I'd try it on with Rebecca when I knew he wanted her. Okay, I've got a rep as a prolific shagger, but I'm always loyal to my mates.

It didn't help that Vicky was angry with me too. She was missing Charlotte and was annoyed that she'd gone because of me. I didn't care what she thought. Me and Charlotte were both single, I'd done nothing wrong.

Besides, Vicky could hardly talk: she was behaving like a right player herself. She was practically cheating on her boyfriend with Ricci. Who did she think she was – me?

Jay and I sorted things out, and he was on my side by the time Vicky finally decided to tell me off. So as far as I was concerned, everything was fine.

Soon after, we all went out for Sophie's birthday. Everyone

agreed to put any bad feelings aside and have fun – we called a truce.

Surprisingly, I found myself actually missing Charlotte. Things just weren't the same without her. She was always the life and soul of the party, and there was definitely a Charlotte-shaped hole in the house.

We all wanted her back, and it looked like the only way she'd return was if I went and got her myself.

So I did.

She looked really refreshed when I picked her up, like the time away from us all had done her the world of good. She'd had a bit of a makeover too – a haircut and a spray tan. I brought her back to the house and everyone was pleased to see her.

I was so glad she was back. I guess I hadn't really realised how much I cared about her until she was gone. She was actually a big part of my life and I started to think that maybe we could work as a couple.

In what was obviously a moment of madness, I suggested that maybe we should actually give it a go and see how things went. She wasn't entirely convinced, but she came into the fuck hut with me anyway and we got it on. I took it to mean that she'd agreed.

We were like rabbits for the next couple of days, and it was nice not to have to go out trawling the clubs to get laid. The parsnip had it on a plate – what could be better than that?

There were some interesting moments during that short spell of calm between us. Charlotte did fart and piss herself when we were getting it on sometimes. It may have been a passion-killer, but it was hilarious.

But then on Vicky's birthday, Charlotte saw Ricci treating

Vicky like a princess and started having a go at me, saying I wasn't as nice to her. I couldn't catch a break.

Ricci's mentality was that 'if you want the gash, you've got to splash the cash'. I was more 'treat them mean, keep them keen'...

She got into a strop and it marked the end of our nice little temporary shagfest.

We threw a house party for Vicky, and Charlotte began flirting with one of Ricci's mates, Leroy, which was fine by me. It gave me a free pass for the weekend and finally made it clear to me that we were mates who sometimes shagged. End of story.

The party was going smoothly, which was surprising for us. But then Ricci got mortal and began annoying everyone.

He boldly announced over the tannoy that he and Vicky were finally a couple, then kept interrupting Jay when he was trying to shag a lass in one of the bedrooms. He was absolutely steaming and it was irritating.

Charlotte started snogging Leroy, which I wasn't bothered about at all. It meant she was finally moving on, and I was pleased I was free. But for some reason Ricci kept goading me about them – trying to get a rise out of me about it. Eventually it all kicked off between us, and while everyone else was still partying, our argument turned physical.

Things started to get smashed and broken and the production staff had to get involved in breaking us up. In the end, James managed to end our fight and we went to bed to sleep it off.

The next morning, we both woke up remorseful and wanting to make up. But Anna, our boss, was there and she was not happy.

She told us it was disgusting behaviour and we knew she was right. We both promised her it would never happen again and said how genuinely sorry we were. Me and Ricci were mates. We couldn't figure out how we had ended up like that.

'It won't happen again, you're right,' she said. 'You're out of this house.'

What? My heart instantly sank and Ricci looked devastated too. But she was serious.

We packed our bags and left, feeling utterly stupid. I'd bonded with all these people and now I had to leave without even saying goodbye. I couldn't believe it was over.

Looking back, it's hard to describe how I felt back then.

I'm not a fighter. I've always shied away from using my fists, especially because I know it's not worth it. But when people are staggering around, slurring their words, sometimes there is no talking to them. And things can get out of control before you even realise what's going on.

I'm still ashamed of what happened back then, and I was so sad to be sent home over something that started out so small. I didn't know what was going to happen next and I felt like a deflated balloon.

We all had to learn how to resolve our conflicts. When you're in the real world you can physically leave a situation that you can see is escalating. You can take time to cool off, put things in perspective, and then maybe call or text to sort things out from a safe distance.

In that house you can't escape. It's taught me a lot about talking things through and making up after fights quickly, so that the conflict doesn't go on and on. In some ways it's a good thing. You get things sorted out right away because there's no other way to do it. But it makes things very awkward at the time.

Eventually we were allowed back into the house and I was so relieved to walk through that door. I said hello to everyone and took my time unpacking, trying to figure out what the situation would now be like with Charlotte.

I spoke to her about things but she seemed to have decided that we should stay away from each other to avoid any more drama. I respected her decision.

Me and Ricci were fine – it was like nothing had ever happened between us. But of course, I got it on with Charlotte again. It was inevitable. We were both suckers for punishment.

The lads decided to go out without the girls one night, so we went to a strip club. It was a laugh, but we came home alone – and found the girls screaming and chanting on the tables and the house in an absolute state. There was mud, chocolate sauce and even a chair in the hot tub. It was like a bunch of wild animals had gone berserk in the place.

For some reason, the girls had absolutely trashed our home while we were out, because they were expecting us to bring the strippers back. It was madness. Of course, we went mental at the girls. And they went mental at us.

Once more we went to bed deeply divided.

The next day, tensions were high. We wanted the girls to apologise for their behaviour, but they wouldn't. So we went golfing instead, and left them at home.

That afternoon, our boss, Anna, called and said we'd be split into two teams to do our spray-tanning jobs. It meant we had to work with the girls – something we weren't looking forward to at all. It would be awkward as fuck.

FAME AND FORTUNE

The lasses put marigolds on and decided to clean up before Anna arrived, which was a good start to their apology. And although it was uncomfortable, we managed to be civil and get our work done. It actually helped I guess, because when we all went out that night things were kind of back to normal, which was a relief.

When our second stint together came to an end, we'd all made peace with each other. And by the time we began packing our bags we were getting emotional again. We may have all fought and screamed at each other but there was a bond of love between us really. I'd miss everyone when they were gone.

As Jay said: 'We are the most dysfunctional, incestuous family there could possibly be. But do you know what? I wouldn't change it for the fucking world.'

PARSNIP POINTERS

NO. 14: THE LONG GAME

It's always good to have a couple of girls in reserve, because you can't always guarantee that you're going to pull on a night out.

This is where playing the long game comes in handy. It's all about putting in the groundwork days, maybe even weeks, beforehand. And man does it pay off.

On some nights out there are so many hot birds around it can seem a shame to waste them all. So don't.

Make eye contact with one and smile at her. If she smiles back, don't approach: wait a while, giving her a few winning grins in the meantime.

When you go over, have a laid-back chat with her and buy her a drink. Don't ask for her number, just ask her if she's having a good night and keep things simple. Don't come on too strong.

Then wish her a good night and walk away.

She'll be confused, which is exactly what you want. Why didn't you pull her, she'll wonder, and come to the conclusion that you're a nice guy.

The next time you bump into her you're practically friends, so it won't be difficult to strike up a conversation again. And you'll have rejected her already, which will make her want you even more.

You can either keep her 'on ice' for another time by walking away again, or take advantage of the fruits of your previous labour if there's no other talent around, and take her home.

This is the long game, and the beauty of it is that you can have as many girls on ice at the same time as you like. That way, you have numerous backups for those sparser nights out...

CHAPTER 15

A CHRISTMAS TO REMEMBER

When filming finally finished on Series Two, I had little time to rest and recover because my agent had lined up a long string of personal appearances. I employed my mate Billy as my driver, and set about making as much money as I could off the back of my new-found fame.

Don't get me wrong, it wasn't always a walk in the park. I definitely put my all into it. I posed for hundreds of photos with fans, I never turned anyone away if they wanted a chat and, of course, I banged a shitload of girls.

The clubs definitely got their money's worth.

Now that I had cash in my account, I was determined to make sure that Christmas 2011 was a time to remember. At this time a year ago I'd been a miserable mess: on the dole with nothing to look forward to. And Mam had been at rock-bottom too, with no money and no house.

As I shopped for everyone's presents, I remembered how she

had cried over not being able to give us special gifts and a memorable day.

I couldn't believe how much both our lives had changed in the past 12 months. Mam was living with George and was blissfully happy. I was now pretty much famous and making serious money at last. I wanted to splash out – to make this Christmas extra special. I bought Mam a beautiful gold bracelet and necklace, my sister an expensive watch, for Grandad I got Formula One tickets, and I paid for a holiday for Dad. I felt like Santa Claus.

I also proudly offered to pay Grandad rent, now that I could afford to. But he told me not to bother. The way he saw it, I was hardly ever at home because I was travelling the country making so many personal appearances. He would feel bad taking my money, he said.

The cast also got involved in playing a little joke on the media when we announced that we were launching our own kebab-scented perfume. It smelled vile – just like a real kebab – but we took it round the newspapers and magazines, promoting it as if it was real. It was such a fun publicity stunt, and we thought it perfectly summed up the whole show.

Over the next few months, while Series Two aired, me and Billy had the time of our lives. We were on the road every single day between venues, partying at night, getting paid for it, then taking girls back to our hotel and partying there too.

I got very little sleep.

Plus I was making thousands of pounds a week, but spending at least a third of it on having a good time. I'll admit I got swept away with the excitement of it all and wasn't very sensible. But it felt so good to have money and I loved splashing out on myself and my mates.

A CHRISTMAS TO REMEMBER

It looked like *Geordie Shore* was popular, so I was sure there would always be more work. I knew they were planning another season, and I waited for the call that would tell me when I should pack my bags again.

But when the call came, I was in for a shock. Apparently MTV weren't sure they wanted me to be part of the next series. There had been some serious discussions about whether I was right for the future of the show.

I'd had that bust-up with Ricci, and they'd heard tales about some slightly wayward antics on the road while I was doing the PAs (Personal Appearances). Yes, I was drinking heavily, sleeping with lots of girls and splashing the cash – I wasn't exactly being sensible, I know. But I was hardly a liability.

It was a huge wake-up call. If I wasn't going to be on the show anymore, I would eventually run out of money. And I was spending it like water, so it wouldn't last long at all.

I panicked. I'd not even had time to get used to my new, exciting life yet, and now it could all end. What would I do next? I hadn't thought about the future for a single second.

It made me realise that this bubble I was living in couldn't last forever. I needed to start saving and investing my money – not throwing it all away on birds and booze and nights out. There would come a time where I wasn't flavour of the month anymore. I wasn't bothered about not being in the limelight, but having no money would be seriously worrying.

I'd be right back to square one again.

For the time being, there was nothing I could do. I waited, nervously, for the decision from high up...

Finally, whoever had to make the final decision agreed I could be on the show. It was a close call: I had nearly lost it all.

GAZ (AND MY PARSNIP)

I promised myself that things would change when I returned from the next stint. Then I put it all to one side and packed my bags once again.

As I made my way to the *Geordie Shore* house for the next round of filming, I made another decision: I would stay away from Charlotte. For two seasons we had been on and off, and I was sick of the hassle of it all. And my thinking was that if I was sick of it, then the viewers must be getting sick of it too. So my plan was to focus on shagging as many birds as possible, and just have a good time. I didn't want any drama. Drama could get me kicked off the show – that much had been made perfectly clear to me.

Arriving at the warehouse gaff that we had last called home just a few months before, I was so glad to see everyone again. Our odd little gang were back together, and we were all buzzing.

Then our boss, Anna, turned up to tell us what our job would be this season. 'I need you to housesit for me,' she said. 'In Mexico.'

We all started screaming. A month in Mexico? Bring it on!

After we'd stopped yelling and hugging each other, Anna explained what would happen. We were going to spend the next month in Cancun, a popular resort for Spring Break – which meant it would be packed with sexy American students, all of whom would be ready to party.

It was going to be mint and I couldn't wait to get on the plane.

Now it was time to take the parsnip abroad again.

Vicky and Jay were booked on a later flight than the rest of us, so when we first arrived at the villa in Cancun, they were not there. The villa was absolutely huge – and we had double beds for the first time. At first we were pleased, but it did mean there was one problem: we would have to share beds, which could obviously get a bit messy when we started bringing birds back.

It was going to be hilarious.

Ricci moped about a bit, obviously missing Vicky, but Rebecca was pleased she wasn't there. They'd fallen out so badly that for her it was nice to have a chance to get to know everyone, without Vicky around to cause tension.

Cancun Chris, our temporary new boss, arrived to give us the lowdown on what we would be doing. He explained we would be looking after the house, doing odd jobs for him, and definitely – most importantly – leaving his tequila alone.

On the first night, he told Rebecca and Charlotte to stay at home, but they didn't listen and defiantly came out with us anyway. I don't think anyone was a fan of Cancun Chris.

Spring Break was mental. Thousands of people were packed into the huge Cancun clubs, and all of them were sweaty and horny. It would be a challenge. In the UK I had the girls sussed, but I reckoned American girls would need to be chatted up differently.

I would have to adapt – learn the ways of the Yanks.

But I was more than up for it, and it didn't take me long to pull an American bird. They were everywhere, all in high spirits and ready for fun. It was literally one of the best nights of my life.

When we got back from that first night out, Vicky and Jay had arrived and while Ricci and Vicky threw themselves into each other's arms, Jay announced he had a girlfriend. What? He was my wingman. He couldn't abandon me.

Maybe I felt a bit vulnerable, because suddenly all my plans about staying away from Charlotte went up in smoke. I tried to pull her, jumping on her in bed – but she wouldn't have it.

'It's been lovely knowing ya,' she said. 'Have a nice sleep.'

And that was it. Oh well. I knew the score now. And there were plenty of lasses to take my mind off it. Beach parties in the day, clubs at night – it would be heaven.

Plus, I'd already figured out that the American girls didn't take nearly as much effort to chat up as the girls I was used to back home – they actually cracked on to us. It was mind-blowing.

Hormones were flying around and everyone wanted to shag with no strings attached. It was the perfect set of conditions for a world-class player to show off their pulling prowess. Who cared whether Charlotte had sacked me off – the parsnip was going international.

Cancun was amazing. We went on yachts, swam in the crystal-clear blue ocean, had plenty of new lasses to play with – I honestly wished it would never end.

But bizarrely, it seemed like the battle of the couples would be the thing that defined our trip to Cancun and I very quickly found myself feeling grateful that I was single. Sophie and her boyfriend Joel, Ricci and Vicky – it was like they were trying to prove who was more in love or something. What the fuck? It was Spring Break, we were supposed to be shagging around and partying, not acting out some kind of epic romance novel. And there was temptation everywhere, which was bound to cause problems.

We'd never really taken to Sophie's cockney boyfriend Joel – we thought he was just trying to mug her off. He was an awful flirt and as much as we wanted to, we just didn't believed he cared about her. We wanted Sophie to be happy and we had previously often got mad at him for messing her around.

This was because we all thought he was only with her to get on telly – at times it seemed like it was so obvious. But when he arrived in Cancun I decided to give him a chance for Sophie's sake, so I had a word with him. I told him he needed to prove himself to Sophie and to us, and then we'd accept him. He had a lot to prove, but at least after our chat he knew the score.

Charlotte decided she was going to be my wingwoman, now that Jay had a girlfriend – and James was on crutches. He'd damaged his knee during a wrestling lesson at the start of our trip, and was finding it hard to get around.

I was fine about my new 'wingwoman'. I had always loved spending time with Charlotte, she was always such a laugh. And when we weren't arguing, she was like my best mate.

On the first night of her new role we went out together to a banging club, and at first things went really well. She was kissing loads of lads and pointing out fit girls for me to pull. It was mint.

But then she got drunk. Which in turn made her get jealous. And I knew it was all going to go wrong.

Every time I started chatting to a girl she'd butt in, all innocent, and chat to them about how much of a slag I was. But she was saying it in a sickly sweet way, like, 'He loves girls like you, he shags them all the time...'

Not the actions of a top-class wingwoman.

So I got pissed off, and she could see it, which only made the situation worse. Suddenly she turned into psycho Charlotte and she launched herself at me, her arms and legs flailing. We ended up scrapping in the club in front of everyone.

I didn't know how I was going to deal with her – she was acting out of control. I didn't want anyone to get hurt, least of all her, but she was like a wild animal. We weren't together – she knew that, I knew that – so why wouldn't she accept it?

She was the one who had offered me her wingwoman services. If she didn't feel she could deal with seeing me with other lasses, why on earth did she think that helping me to pull them was such a great idea?

I went home alone and went straight to bed, in a foul mood.

For the rest of the month I tried to keep my distance, and was happy when she eventually starting pulling lads. I wasn't at all jealous of the lads she got together with – even a lad who Charlotte really liked, called Australian Andy.

She'd first met him at a beach party, when they'd flirted but not shagged, and they'd kept in touch. It was all cool.

We went out clubbing one night to celebrate my birthday and she brought him along. I was determined to enjoy myself and let the parsnip have a good night out. I was turning 24, I was in Cancun, and I was the star of a reality show that was getting amazing ratings. I wanted it to be a night to remember, and I got on it, hard.

I pulled, but I didn't manage to bring anyone back with me, which was disappointing.

But Charlotte did – Australian Andy.

It pissed me off a bit if I'm honest.

Everyone thought I was just trying to hide my feelings for Charlotte, but I wasn't. I honestly wasn't bothered about her shagging someone else. I loved her as a mate, but I knew we would never work as a couple. It was Charlotte who kept changing her mind about how she felt.

But I was annoyed that I didn't have a bird to shag on my

birthday. It was petty but that's how I felt. So when everyone thought I was jealous, they were right – but I wasn't jealous of Andy. I was just jealous that they were shagging and I wasn't.

Over the next few days I was actually glad when Andy was around – his presence meant I had a free pass and no drama because she was occupied with him.

With most of the gang coupled up – Charlotte banging Andy, James on crutches and Holly playing at being his horny Florence Nightingale – it felt like it was down to me to provide the entertainment and I more than made up for the others. I shagged loads of birds, and showed Cancun a bit of Newcastle charm.

When Andy went back to Oz, Charlotte was on the lookout for a replacement and tried to get it on with me again. But this time I refused. I just wanted the on-again off-again nonsense to stop. Every time I wanted her, she didn't want me, and every time she wanted me, I couldn't be bothered with the hassle.

It was ridiculous. We were behaving like silly teenagers.

We formed an unspoken, uneasy truce. She got on with kissing random lads, and I got on with pulling birds. One night I even managed to pull two lasses at the same time.

I'd kissed them both in a club, and managed to convince both of them to come back to the villa with me.

The three of us shared a few drinks and then crawled into bed, giggling – and just got on with it together.

They were hot Australian lasses and they certainly knew how to please the parsnip. It was the first time that a threesome had been shown on TV – which was a pretty awesome claim to fame. But I knew Charlotte wasn't happy about it, even though she'd pulled a lad that night too.

We were just going round in circles.

GAZ (AND MY PARSNIP)

Overall, we had fun on our Spring Break. And while I was regularly giving into temptation with the lasses, I forced myself not to give in to another huge temptation in Cancun: our boss's precious tequila.

Almost every day I would look up at the top shelf and see the special bottle of booze that Cancun Chris had threatened us over if we ever touched it. I really wanted to drink it. Not because I liked tequila but because I'd been told I couldn't have it. It was like a red rag to a bull.

Eventually the inevitable happened – I got it down and made everyone drink it, so that I wasn't the only perpetrator involved in the crime. We felt like naughty school kids, and couldn't stop laughing as we laid into it. It was hilarious, and it sparked a mini house party. We drank every last drop.

Chris was, as I had anticipated, not impressed. He held me responsible and ordered me to replace it, but it was such a rare bottle that only a few places in Mexico sold it.

I grabbed Charlotte and took her on a hunt for the bottle, which took hours and was actually great fun. At one point we were so hungry we stopped for food in the middle of nowhere. The only place we could find was a tiny backwater shack, where we ate a plate of unidentifiable food – surrounded by hundreds of creepy beetles.

Charlotte couldn't stop screaming. At first I rolled my eyes, but when one crawled up my leg I began squealing too. We bonded over the experience, and I started to soften towards her again, which I knew was a bad idea.

That season was full of bombshells and explosions.

Sophie got emotional and flew home early. Vicky and Ricci got thrown out of the house for arguing, before insanely getting engaged and going back early as well. Me and Charlotte had yet another blazing row and may have thrown a thing or two around the villa, which didn't go down well at all with anyone. She kept getting jealous when I pulled girls and it was seriously cramping my style.

It was an impossible situation. We knew we both needed to call a real truce in order to move forwards, but it was so difficult. We just kept hurting each other. The problem was, when things were good between us they were so good. But when they were bad they were awful. I could only hope that it wouldn't last forever.

The weather was amazing, the villa was incredible and we should have been having the best time ever. But the constant arguments were stressful and it felt oddly overwhelming. We were knackered, which didn't help our mood a lot of the time, and half our group left, which made things seem very weird. The relentless partying was fun, but looking back on it maybe it was too much fun. Towards the end we seriously started to run out of steam, although we all kept going because we wanted to make the most of it all.

At times it really felt like we were in a pressure cooker. We couldn't get away from each other and kept exploding. As I've explained before, there was no release valve – no chance to escape each other and gather our thoughts.

I had decided not to sleep with Charlotte in Cancun, thinking it would sort things out between us, and on the whole I'd been successful in my resolve. But staying out of her pants had actually made things worse. I didn't want to lose her as a friend. She was irreplaceable. But what could I do?

I was well and truly tired of it all.

On Jay's birthday, which was close to the end of the trip, we decided to stay in and have a barbeque at the villa. We all wanted a change from the relentless clubbing, and needed a quiet night for once.

It was a nice, relaxing evening – everyone was finally getting on again and everything was chilled. But then Jay dropped a massive bombshell: he was leaving the show, to really make things work with his girlfriend, Chloe.

I was shocked into speechlessness. The girls started crying, and I soon joined them. I was gutted. Truly gutted. Jay was my best mate in the house and now he was leaving me. Ricci and Vicky were gone, after being boring all through the holiday, Sophie had got overwhelmed and flown home and now Jay was off. Everyone was dropping like flies. What was happening to us?

In fact I couldn't imagine not having Jay around. He was the only one I could turn to, the only one that I was truly close to. He was my rock. I didn't know how I was going to carry on myself without him. I forgot all about the cameras and just wept. It was an awful end to the holiday.

At least I would be flying back in comfort, courtesy of James's broken leg. His insurance company was paying for him to fly business class on the way home, and had said he could take one of us with him. He had picked me. Way-fucking-ay.

But I didn't know what the future would bring when I returned to the UK and the reality of everyday life. Flying back, I knew I had to sort myself out financially. It was time to get serious. It was time to formulate a plan.

PARSNIP POINTERS

NO. 15: ENTERTAIN HER

When you're chatting up a girl, it can sometimes be difficult to know what to say to keep the conversation flowing in the right direction.

It's easy to resort to asking her a never-ending stream of questions to show her how interested you are. But this can be tiring for both of you, and even make you look a little desperate.

You have to try to strike a nice balance between asking about her and talking about yourself, which is no easy thing.

To make sure you're prepared, you should work on having a few reserve statements, stories and jokes up your sleeve, so that you can come across as confident and funny even if the conversational well has run dry.

It's important to keep updating these little nuggets to keep them fresh too. You don't want it to sound like you've told this same story a hundred times, you want it to come out as though it's literally just popped into your head. Changing up your stories and jokes will keep them original and relevant.

And steer clear from too many tales about your drunken antics. Regaling her with a story about the time that you and your mate Joe vomited in a neighbour's plant pot on the way home from a club won't score you any points.

CHAPTER 16

PLANNING
AHEAD

Back in Newcastle, it was nice to have some peace and quiet. I caught up with my family and friends, and had a well-deserved break. Then, in preparation for Series Three going live, we began to promote the show again – doing interviews and photo shoots, and going to premieres and celebrity events. It was great to get back to what was by now a sort of familiar routine.

I went on tour again, doing personal appearances in clubs all over the UK. But although I was making money, I wasn't completely happy with my management.

There was a lot of money being deducted from my pay, which I couldn't understand. I knew that they had to make money out of me too, but the percentages seemed to be very high. I was doing most of the hard work, after all. It was me who was on the road every day and playing up to the club crowds at night. It was me who was surviving on little sleep and succumbing to exhaustion-related illnesses all the time.

I wondered whether I could get a better deal elsewhere.

Holly was with a different management company from the one the rest of us were with, and so I thought I'd try my luck with them instead.

With this new company, all the personal appearances were being organised by a guy called Shaq, and I instantly got on with him. He was fun but dedicated, and quickly booked me up solid for months. He was working with another great guy called Kay, and, between the three of us, in no time at all we were working hard and raking in the cash.

Eventually Shaq and Kay came to me with a proposition: they wanted to manage me fully themselves. At first I wasn't sure.

They were in charge of organising PAs and after-parties, which they did brilliantly well, but I didn't know whether they could handle the other things agents do.

I decided to take a chance, and in hindsight it was the best decision I could ever have made. They created IMA Management, and took complete charge of my career. Two years on, we're still an exceptional team. They're truly brilliant agents. And they're like family to me.

When they took me on, I confided in them how I'd felt when I was nearly chucked off the show before Cancun.

'I was shitting myself,' I said. 'I need to make myself financially secure. I'll work harder than you've ever seen, just book me everywhere you can.'

So we decided to set ourselves a target: it was March 2012, which meant there were nine months before the next Christmas. 'I want to have a six-figure sum in my account before Christmas,' I told them.

We shook on it. It was time to get down to some serious work.

PLANNING AHEAD

When Series Three aired, my Twitter followers nearly doubled to over a million. Everyone wanted a piece of me, and there was plenty to go around. With Billy, who was still my driver, Shaq and Kay by my side, we stormed the UK's clubs, getting paid tens of thousands to do so.

I did 45 PAs, had two days off, then did another 50 in a row. It was exhausting and I got so ill. I had mouth ulcers all the time, and got pretty unhealthy. But I was determined not to quit. I'd set myself a challenge and I was going to achieve it.

Besides, it was good fun, mostly.

I pulled loads of birds, sometimes having six or seven back in my room at one time. One night I brought so many back that they had to queue up outside my room, while I banged them one by one inside. The parsnip was becoming legendary, and my bank account was certainly looking very healthy by the time we began filming Series Four.

This time, we were back in Newcastle. And with no Jay, and also no Rebecca – because she'd decided to leave too – we had new people to meet.

While we caught up over a few drinks as usual, Charlotte surprised us all by saying she had a boyfriend. I was pleased. Maybe this time we could concentrate on being mates and not have the drama that had been so unhealthy and disruptive in the past.

So with Holly, Charlotte, Sophie, James, Ricci and Vicky all standing around having a drink with me, we were impatient to meet our new housemates. I hoped that any lad that came in would be game for a laugh – someone I could go out pulling with and get to know well.

And if there was a bird, well, I could only hope that they were fit. The first newbie to turn up was Scott Timlin. As soon as he bounded through the door with his big Cheshire grin, I just knew he'd be sound. We were even wearing the same top!

As he ran his mouth off about what a pulling legend he was, everyone thought that I'd finally met my match – but I knew I had found a running mate for the season. I couldn't wait to get pulling with my new dream team in place. We would do some serious damage together.

Our other newbie, Dan Thomas-Tuck, arrived soon after and so with the new house at maximum capacity we started to get smashed to celebrate our first night as housemates.

Dan got absolutely slaughtered, and so did Charlotte. They got in the hot tub together and Dan drunkenly started to try it on with her, which she didn't seem impressed with.

I was inside with Scott and the other lads, but Vicky came and told me what was going on and I was instantly concerned.

Charlotte had a boyfriend and although we weren't together I still cared about her. I didn't want to see her get hurt and I could see this new guy was getting in her face about something or other. No matter what had happened between us in the past, I was always going to protect her. So I went to keep an eye on things. I quickly saw that he was behaving like a right knob, and I wasn't happy.

I told him to back off and we had an argument. I ended up giving him a shove and then walking off to calm down. Everyone was confused about why I was angry, but I was just looking out for Charlotte.

It wasn't a good start. Ding ding! It was the first night and Round One had already kicked off.

Dan spent most of the rest of the night vomiting his guts up, and the girls had to help him out before I eventually carried him to bed. He hadn't made the best first impression, but I hoped it was just because he was excited and had got absolutely mortal without realising it.

The next day he dutifully apologised and we decided to give him the benefit of the doubt. Despite what it may seem, we're not always drinking during our time filming – as viewers, you only see a very small amount of the time that we're together, and we only really drink when we're going out to party.

Most of the time we're completely sober.

We'd all made prats of ourselves at some point during our time in the house; it was just unfortunate that Dan had done it on his first night with everyone.

Putting it all behind us, we went out to the horse races for Ladies Day. We were suited and booted, and the girls were dolled up too. We looked hot to trot. Ladies Day? Its very name surely meant we would pull.

When we got there, it was absolutely rammed with worldies. I couldn't believe I'd never gone there before – it was the perfect pulling ground. I don't know anything about tips for the races themselves, but my tip would definitely be to GO to the races.

Over the next few days my new 'dream team' worked as well as I hoped it would: on nights out, me and Scott were perfect pulling partners and were snogging birds left, right and centre. Scott even got it on with Holly, which meant he always had someone to shag if he didn't bring a girl back. I liked his style.

One night both me and Scott both brought lasses back to the house. But weirdly, Charlotte tried to stop me from shagging mine. She had a boyfriend now – what did she think she was doing?

She kept coming into the fuck hut and interrupting me and

my lass before we could really get going. It was frustrating, but it actually worked out for the best in the end – Scott and his lass got into the bed with me and mine and we ended up having a foursome.

As we hi-fived over the two girls I silently thanked Charlotte. If she hadn't come in we would have been done by the time Scott turned up with his bird.

I wasn't sure how much Charlotte was really bothered about her boyfriend if she was still getting jealous of the girls I was shagging.

I was intrigued about meeting him, and it wasn't long before I had the opportunity to. We threw an engagement party for Ricci and Vicky, and Charlotte invited him along.

We had a champagne fountain, classy decorations, and all the girls were bringing their female mates. Me and Scott agreed we were going to smash it and joked about who would do better.

It was great to have a bit of friendly competition to spice things up. I always work my magic better when I've got someone to beat, and Scott was exactly the same. It was mint.

The party was in full swing when Charlotte's boyfriend, also called Scott, turned up. Despite my initial intrigue about him, I decided I just wanted him to stay out of my way. There was actually no need for us to get to know each other. Everything would be fine if we didn't cross paths. I just wanted to have fun and there were plenty of lasses to keep me occupied. Luckily he got himself smashed before we had the chance to run into each other, and Charlotte had to put him to bed early.

What a relief that was. But he wouldn't go to sleep and they ended up having an argument in the early hours of the morning. For some unknown reason she had told him she hadn't missed him, which had obviously pissed him off. He was walking around naked, screaming at her at the top of his lungs, and everyone could hear.

I was in the middle of banging a cute blonde when I heard the sound of things getting smashed. The argument was obviously escalating, and I didn't know what to do – should I carry on shagging or get up and investigate what was going on?

I decided it was best not to get involved. I didn't want a punch-up, nor did I want to get into trouble. Too many cooks spoil the broth, as they say, and similarly too many people getting in on an argument can only escalate it out of control.

Luckily Scott left, but the arguments kept raging – this time between Charlotte and Vicky.

Charlotte had heard Ricci slagging her off, saying that she was an idiot for saying what she'd said. But when Charlotte began to whine about Ricci, Vicky stepped in to defend her man.

It was mental.

Suddenly everyone was yelling at everyone. It was a complete disaster and I was so grateful I'd kept my head down.

When we woke up the following morning, all of us were silent as we cleaned up the flat. We'd all been through a lot together on the show, but this was the biggest argument that had occurred, and I didn't know what would happen next. The atmosphere was pretty awful. Everyone was too scared to say anything to anyone, in case things kicked off again.

Anna arrived and we knew we were in for a telling off. She ordered Vicky, Ricci and Sophie to leave the house for a while

– we'd only been there for a few days! And Charlotte's boyfriend wasn't allowed in the house ever again.

I did feel sorry for her, but it was good news for me. I just wanted to hang out with the new guy Scott and get on with partying. But we were all so down and we needed cheering up, so those of us who were left decided to go to the beach for some fresh air.

I took the opportunity to speak to Charlotte. Because I'd stayed out of it all, I didn't know exactly what had happened, but Charlotte didn't really understand either, so she couldn't shed much light on things.

The thing is, I didn't want Charlotte to feel it was her fault. She was really down and I told her to stop worrying. She couldn't help it if her boyfriend had been a dick.

We slowly picked up the pieces. Vicky came back but wasn't in the mood to party, so she mostly moped around the house. The other six of us went out to Middlesbrough to see Holly's old stomping ground, and had a really great time. But I still wanted everything to go back to normal, and with Ricci and Sophie still gone, everything felt weird.

Were we always going to argue? Could we not just get along? We had an amazing opportunity – we were on telly, were really making a name for ourselves, and our futures all looked bright. But all these bust-ups had the potential to ruin it all and it was very worrying.

I spent most of my time that season with Scott. We were both laid-back, both on the same page, and we got on so well.

All we wanted to do was have fun with no drama, and so that's what we did. We got on with our token jobs – that season it was massaging people – went out to party at night, and pulled a load of birds. The Buck Squad was born.

PLANNING AHEAD

But not everyone was happy with our teamwork, and the girls decided to form their own gang, the Cockblock Crusaders, to try and stop us bringing lasses back all the time.

In fact, they did have some limited success – but only because they generally got drunk and needed us to take them home.

Charlotte crawled into my bed on one of those nights. Although I was tempted to bang her, I didn't want to ruin her relationship, so I moved to Ricci's bed, which at that point was still empty.

Why couldn't she just move on?

Ricci and Sophie finally came back and we all agreed to make a fresh start. Things were awkward at first, but we knew we had to push past it if we were going to be one big happy family again, which was, deep down, what we all wanted.

It felt like it would be impossible, but we knew we had to give it a go. James decided to organise a team-building activity, and took us all Segway riding round a specially made track. It was hilarious – like riding a little hoover on wheels.

In the spirit of reconciliation, Sophie said sorry to Vicky and asked if they could move on. But Vicky wouldn't accept her apology and had a face liked a smacked arse for the whole day. But most importantly, I had the fastest time round the Segway track out of everyone. I ignored Vicky's scowls and was buzzing the whole day.

As the weeks passed, everyone else made up and got on with having a good time. But we couldn't escape the drama. Charlotte's boyfriend broke up with her, Joel was still hanging around Sophie, annoying us all, and Vicky and Ricci had an endless stream of arguments, which culminated in Ricci asking for Vicky's engagement ring back.

Eventually they both left the house to save their relationship and I was glad. It wasn't healthy having them around. It felt like the air was poisonous.

Then things started to prove problematic between me and Charlotte – again. All the lads were being auctioned off for charity one night, and although Charlotte bid on me, she didn't win.

Later on, she flirted with me and tried to get into my bed, before Sophie intervened and made her sleep on the floor instead. It was for the best – starting up again would only cause problems. But I could tell she was upset.

Leaving the house at the end of our time together, we all felt completely rubbish. Dan had got upset with me and Scott for 'leaving him out' and Holly had confessed undying love for James.

They'd had their casual little fling in Cancun, but while Holly was still harbouring feelings for him, James was loved up with a girlfriend, so it didn't go down well.

We all felt deflated as we packed for home, and I didn't say much as I kissed Charlotte goodbye and left.

This had been our toughest time together yet. The arguments and emotions flying around had been emotionally draining. Watching your friends argue is never fun, and we felt like we were so much more than friends. It hurt when we all fell out.

It had been a blast, and I still maintained I had the best job ever. But for now we all definitely needed the time away from each other.

PARSNIP POINTERS

NO. 16: MAKE AN EFFORT WITH YOUR APPEARANCE

Just like you would rather chat up a girl who had taken the time to doll herself up for the night, lasses are much more drawn to a guy who clearly looks after himself.

Always shower and shave before you go out, and spritz yourself all over with a good aftershave. Wear clean clothes, even down to your shoes, and make sure your hair is neat and tidy too.

Brush your teeth as well. The last thing you want is to go over and give a lass your winning smile, only to see her recoil in horror because there's something stuck between your gnashers.

Also, bad breath is just about the most instant turn-off in the world, so make sure you've got a stick of chewing gum handy.

Finally, do a few sit-ups and press-ups before you leave for the night. It'll temporarily pump up your pecs a bit more and we all know how girls like to see a bit of muscle. Just remember this helpful army motto: perfect preparation prevents piss poor performance…

CHAPTER 17

PROJECT 722 IS BORN

Back in the real world, I returned to my master plan to make as much money as possible. I'd set myself the target of making a six-figure sum by Christmas 2012 and after filming Series Four it was now already September and I still had a way to go yet.

I pushed myself to the absolute limit. I found myself in a different city every day, a different club every night, and I hardly took any time off at all. I managed to do 56 personal appearances in 60 days and I was constantly exhausted. I was making money and having the time of my life, but despite the fact that my plan was working I knew I had to think bigger.

It was obvious that I couldn't keep on with this lifestyle forever – I'd burn out. No one could handle that kind of physical strain on their body. I would make money, my bulging bank account was already evidence of that. But I would only make a limited amount before I would have to stop for the sake of my health.

Slowly, as I moved from town to town, another idea formed.

I was still getting sent free T-shirts to promote other people's products by wearing them. I had over a million followers on Twitter – if even only a thousand of them bought the T-shirts I was wearing, that added up to a hefty chunk of cash that I was making for free, for other people.

Why shouldn't I have a piece of that action?

A friend of mine, Andrew Hayton, had a small clothes shop in Newcastle, so I had a word with him on one of my rare days off, and we formed a plan. We would open our own shop together, since everyone loved my style so much. With my name backing the shop, it was sure to be a winner.

I couldn't wait – this was the way I was going to make my fortune and secure my finances for the future. Whatever life would bring, if this new venture worked I was going to be set up for life.

We scouted out a location, and found the perfect place – in the Newcastle Metro Centre. I could hardly believe how things had turned out.

As we excitedly began to kit out the huge space, I felt like my life had come full circle. I had painstakingly tiled this place as a lad, and now I would be one of the lucky people who owned a shop here. I'd envied those people so much back in my college days.

In my head, they'd made a success out of their lives and I never dreamed I'd one day be able to count myself among them.

I called in some of my old workmates from that time and said: 'Lads, do you want a job? Come and tile my new shop...'

It felt so good – I was standing in the bare bones of my own business, watching the guys I used to work with help me to get it ready for trading.

We got a website designer to build us a virtual shop site as well, so that at some point we could start to do online sales too. Me and my new business partner worked long hours together to design our business. We picked the staff and chose the stock and decided that it was going to be a proper lads' playground inside. We made it into something really special, and I'm so proud of it.

Great music, awesome clothes and entertainment while you shop – Project 722 was born.

The best thing about it was that I knew it would be a really fun environment. I was determined to make sure there were always prizes up for grabs to get people through the door – to reflect my own competitive nature. So we planned to have *FIFA* and *Call of Duty* tournaments going on every Saturday. It was an inspired decision.

I wanted it to be the kind of shop I'd want to visit myself and I was determined to make it a success. So I decided not to take a wage from it for at least a year. This was my long-term project. It needed time to grow before it bore me the fruit I planned on harvesting.

Around the country, millions of *Geordie Shore* fans were tuning in to see me entertain them with my endless pulling and constant partying, but in reality I was being as sensible as I possibly could. I had to be shrewd about things if I was going to make my *Geordie Shore* experience work for me. It was a side of me the fans knew nothing about, and something I hoped they eventually would see and respect me for.

By the time we began filming Series Five in October that

year, I was starting to finally feel secure. Now, whatever happened on the show, and however long this amazing bubble lasted, I was going to be okay. I had plans in motion to open my own store, money in the bank and I had my head screwed on right at long last.

I could go back into the house, tear up the town, and have fun. Then when I got out, I would open my store and continue to work hard on my future. I was finally making something of my life.

One by one, we all turned up at the Newcastle house that by now was so familiar to us. Anna arrived once we were all there, and told us that this season we would be travelling all over Europe – for her new hen- and stag-do business, called Geordie Tours. We would be in charge of entertaining the rowdy hens and stags. It would be immense fun.

'Your first stop will be Amsterdam,' she told us.

The sex capital of Europe? Get in.

I still didn't know what was going to happen with Charlotte. Viewers had seen us kiss before we'd left the house in the last season, but we still weren't together. I wanted to make the show as entertaining as possible, which meant going out and making merry mayhem happen. I really saw it as my professional duty. This was my job and I wanted to do it to the best of my ability.

But my soft spot for Charlotte was always causing tension and I couldn't seem to stop myself from being drawn back into something with her.

Even when she had a boyfriend we'd managed to have problems. Now she was single again and I had no idea what would happen. I'd actually really missed her between filming.

I had some big decisions to make.

PROJECT 722 IS BORN

The one decision I had made was to take Dan under my wing this time – he was like a little brother who just wanted to know the ways of the Buck Squad. He'd felt a bit left out of things last time, and although we hadn't meant to make him feel like that I felt it was my duty to include him more.

Me and Scott had bonded so well and so quickly, and Dan had tried so hard to be part of things. Maybe we hadn't really done as much as we could have to involve him. He was a nice lad, so there was no reason for us not to make an effort to include Dan in our exploits.

When we arrived in Amsterdam, me and Scott wasted no time in getting out to the famous red light district. We found a novelty condom shop and couldn't believe the stuff that was in there. We bought the biggest ones we could find to fit our extra large parsnips. I wanted one that said, 'You've been Gazzed', but weirdly they didn't have one...

When we got back to the gang, we handed them out to everyone and Dan immediately put his on his head. I just mouthed 'No', laughing. Poor lad. I had a lot of work to do to get him ready for the Buck Squad.

On our first night in the city we couldn't wait to get out there and smash it. The club we went to was great – the music was bouncing, the birds were fit – and it was exactly what I expected Amsterdam to be like.

I ended up sitting with Charlotte in the club and I stupidly told her how much I fancied her when she was all dolled up. It didn't go down well. She called me superficial and vain. It wasn't a good start, so I went and found myself a random bird to pull and felt much better.

The next day we had to start work – entertaining our first hen party. Me and Scott literally rubbed our hands with glee.

If there was one thing we knew how to do, it was showing girls a good time.

I tried to put Charlotte out of my mind. I fancied her, but I knew if I shagged her again I'd probably have to commit to her. It would mean I'd get less grief in the house, but was it the right thing to do? Would it last? I just wasn't sure.

Sam, Anna's representative in Amsterdam, laid down our working ground rules, warning us not to flirt with the hens or drink any booze. 'You're not here to have a good time,' she said sternly. 'You're here to work.'

We completely ignored her of course. Being in charge of gangs of fit birds, all up for it? This wasn't work, it was heaven. We met up with our hens and immediately got the shots in for everyone. When all the lasses were merry, we decided to go for a *Geordie Shore* record – a six-way kiss. But when it came down to it, we couldn't get all our heads in, so we had to kiss them all separately. What a drag.

It was funny. We'd come all the way to Amsterdam to pull Dutch birds and we'd ended up pulling a load of Brits instead.

I didn't care. This new job was the best ever. I was fully prepared to do the lion's share of the work while we were here.

Like I've said before, I've always been a hard grafter!

After our work was done, we had to go and meet the others to celebrate Vicky's birthday. We arrived at the club a bit merry and still buzzing from our shift, and when I saw Charlotte – looking beautiful – I decided to take a different approach with her.

I left Scott to go it alone and sat down and started being honest with Charlotte. I told her that I really wanted her and asked her to go home with me that night.

But while I was being kind of sincere, she was being all cool and calm, pretending she didn't care about me. 'Any hole's a goal,' she told me. 'Just go and pull, I don't mind.'

Naturally I was a bit taken aback and didn't know how to react. I was so used to just being able to have her. When she turned me down, I was confused. The booze I'd drunk obviously wasn't helping me see things clearly, either. I stuck at it, ignoring the fact that I could see Scott necking with a load of worldies out of the corner of my eye. I'd made a decision and I wanted to see it through. But she was firm. For about a day, anyway.

I skulked off, feeling rejected.

The next night I boldly crawled into her bed – while she was next to Holly, who was fast asleep. We'd all gone out and got mortal drunk, and though Charlotte was still pieing me, I didn't want to give up. She whispered that she still wasn't going to have sex with me, but she clearly didn't mean it. Because five minutes later I was making her moan and scream with pleasure like she always used to.

'What happens in Amsterdam stays in Amsterdam,' I giggled when we'd finished. I still didn't know what was going to happen, but for the time being, I was happy. For me, the ideal would be that we could be shagging buddies until we wanted to settle down. But I'd have to wait and see.

We flew back to Newcastle and waited for the next leg of the Geordie Tour to be announced. Things were calm, even when Joel turned up, looking like a complete bellend in a stars-and-stripes onesie.

Charlotte seemed laid-back about our Dutch shag. I reckoned maybe we had turned a corner. And Charlotte and Holly even formed a new team, calling themselves 'The Cock

Catchers' and challenging The Buck Squad to a pulling contest. I was ready to smash her into the ground. I could definitely pull more birds than she could lads. I was a pro.

We all got ready and headed out to a club. Me and Scott got stuck in, but the girls just looked like fish out of water. It was hilarious. At one point during the night I had a girl either side of me and I was kissing them both, while The Cock Catchers were floundering around, embarrassingly tapping on various lads' shoulders.

This was one contest I wasn't worried about losing.

Later on, Dan turned up with a lass he'd pulled on the hen party job he'd been working. He was looking very pleased with himself. I'd given him some pulling tips and told him to just get on with it, and it looked like he'd taken my advice on board. But when we saw his proud grin and eyed up the girl he'd got with, we began wetting ourselves laughing.

It was mean, but we told him that in all seriousness she wasn't up to our standards. We teased him about it relentlessly, getting meaner and meaner. We saw his face instantly fall, and found it funny that the more we wound him up, the more he blatantly pied her off. Eventually he ran away and hid from her, the poor lass.

Then we lost interest. Besides, me and Scott had problems of our own. We'd pulled a couple of girls and ending up having a four-way kiss, which was all good until we felt our tongues touch each other.

We both recoiled in shock, and fell about laughing. We'd both pulled most of the girls in Newcastle; it was only a matter of time before we ended up pulling each other, I guess!

And we'd been cruel to Dan – the girl wasn't that awful, and we'd only really been winding him up like big brothers.

But he wasn't happy. He felt like there was no pleasing us, I guess.

Next day, Anna told him off about the way he'd treated the girl and made him clean the limo bus as punishment, while we all went go-karting. Poor lad. I didn't feel guilty though. I told myself it was all part of his apprenticeship.

The girls vs boys pulling contest continued over the next few nights, and although they'd started off poorly, they started to actually catch us up. Charlotte was kissing any lad she could find and though it wasn't like her to behave in that way I still thought it was funny.

I didn't like anyone beating me, so I pulled out all the stops and charmed my way through the clubs, ticking off the girls one by one. This was war.

It may have seemed like it was lads vs lasses, but deep down we knew it was really me vs Charlotte. She was trying to prove that she had got over me.

One night, I pulled a girl early in the evening and took her home for a shag. I was getting on with it when the front door open and I heard Charlotte come in with a lad.

I was impressed. She'd brought a guy back and into bed without passing out, being sick or pissing on him.

And we weren't yelling at each other either.

Everything was okay.

Even when she announced the next day that she was going on a date with him I was pleased for her. But maybe, in hindsight, I was a little bit green-eyed. And maybe we were actually trying to make each other jealous with our little pulling contest. People don't always know exactly why they're behaving the way they do.

She took her date to a club, and I saw her kissing him. I

told myself I wasn't bothered and went on a pulling spree. But for some reason I was off my game and I didn't take anyone back home.

Everyone got pissed. And when we got back the obligatory fireworks began. Vicky and Ricci began arguing over some of their usual nonsense and we tried to help sort it out, but it only made things worse. Why don't we ever learn not to get involved?

Suddenly Scott went mental too, for some unknown reason. Holly took control of the situation and gave him a blowjob to calm him down. Eventually the house fell quiet again.

Me and Charlotte were the only ones still up and though we were smashed we were still drinking. Heavy duty flirting ensued and I could see where things were going. I picked her up and carried her to bed. I was very gentlemanly – I even asked her how her date was while we were shagging...

Soon after, we were told we were flying to Prague for our next leg of the Geordie Tour. But on the first night we were there, Charlotte turned psycho again and tried to stop me pulling.

I knew things were going to end badly. I was angry and tired, so I got smashed when we got back to the Prague villa.

Actually, when I say I got smashed, I'm not even half describing how pissed I was. I really got mortal – more than I ever usually do. I downed drink after drink, not caring about my normal need to stay in control.

I started arguing with Charlotte, but I was so drunk I just ended up running to the bathroom and vomiting. It was awful. Usually I was the one who put other people to bed, but I was in a right state and couldn't even help myself. I started calling out Charlotte's name like a kid calling for their mam. But I knew she would look after me and I didn't care that everyone was laughing at me. I was so grateful. She put all our arguing to one side and helped me to bed.

As I snuggled under the covers, I suddenly felt very sentimental and I couldn't help myself from pouring out my drunken feelings. 'I love you,' I told her, as she held me under the covers. 'No you don't,' she said.

But I really did, even if it wasn't the kind of love she wanted or needed. I'd opened myself up to her and she was still rejecting me. It wasn't the best I'd ever felt in my life.

The next morning, I woke up and Charlotte was lying next to me. I felt absolutely minging, but at least I had someone to cuddle. I suddenly felt horny and I asked her to play with my willy. 'I don't want to have sex with you anymore,' she said. 'Me and you are just friends.'

'Yeah, I know that,' I said, secretly still feeling a bit rejected.

I didn't need this. I was in Prague to have a good time and me and Charlotte were back to our usual on-again off-again nonsense. We needed to make up our minds about what we wanted, but it didn't look like that was going to happen any time soon.

She got out of the bed and left me alone with my brutal hangover.

At that point I didn't remember anything about telling Charlotte that I loved her, but as I lay there feeling very sorry for myself I soon started to have flashbacks. 'Ah shit,' I thought.

I still felt the same as I always had – I didn't want to commit to her, no matter how much I felt for her. Telling her I loved her was not the smartest of moves.

As I was lying in my bed, thinking things through, the

phone rang and I was told I had to go on a bar crawl for work.

It was the last thing I needed. Sometimes being on the show could be a real drag. This was one of those moments.

While me, Sophie and Dan went to work, Scott and Charlotte sneaked off alone to have some fun together. They ended up buying stupid furry hats and drinking absinthe in a funny little bar. They got absolutely hammered.

When they got back, they were laughing and joking with each other and I wasn't sure how I felt about them spending so much time together. Things were getting weird again and we inevitably started arguing soon after.

We'd decided to have a family night, which meant no pulling for anyone. We were all just going to enjoy each other's company and have a good time as a group.

But emotions ran high when I saw Charlotte chatting up some lads and I told her I wasn't happy about it. She thought I was messing with her head and started crying again.

By the time we got back home we were all so utterly exhausted that we went to bed for once without a blazing row.

Charlotte and I snuggled up together and just went to sleep. It felt so natural. Maybe we were messing with each other's heads...

All in all, though, Prague was wicked.

I tried traditional Czech dancing, had a bath in beer and apart from my one mega hangover I had an amazing time. We even managed to temporarily drag Ricci away from Vicky and visit some strippers.

Back in the Toon, we settled back into Geordie life once more.

Charlotte started pulling again and I got back into the swing of things myself. I took some much-needed time out to go and see Grandad, and it was good to catch up and have a rest. We went for a walk and I explained everything that had happened with Charlotte. He helped me put things in perspective.

I told him I had always said I wouldn't be with her and I was sticking to it, even though we kept ending up in bed together. 'Well she can't blame you if you sleep with someone else then,' said Grandad.

It was the truth. If he could see the situation, then I definitely wasn't being an arsehole, was I? Just because I cared about her, it didn't change the fact that I wasn't ready to have a relationship – with anyone. Charlotte knew that it wasn't personal. I just wasn't in the right place to have a serious committed relationship.

I went back to the house and gave her a little bell I'd bought in Prague, as a sort of peace gesture. I wanted to show her that I'd always be around if she needed me, despite the fact we weren't together. I jokingly told her that all she had to do was ring the bell and I'd be there.

But she took it as far more of a romantic gesture than I meant it to be. I was trying to be sweet but it backfired. It wasn't long before psycho Charlotte made her return in spectacular fashion.

We went out clubbing that night and I was getting it on with a hot girl, when all of a sudden, Charlotte came storming over.

'If you have sex with that girl I won't ever speak to you again,' she said, raging. I was amazed. It was emotional blackmail. She'd just been on a date herself and now she was telling me to stay away from lasses? The anger I felt was uncontrollable. 'It's desperate man, why are you doing it?' she went on.

She thought I was only trying to pull a girl to make her jealous because she had gone on a date. Did she even know me? I pulled girls all the time. Tonight was no different from any other night.

But I'd given her that stupid bell which apparently meant I'd declared undying love for her. I was tired of it all and was pleased when she stormed off in a huff and went home.

When the rest of us came back a few hours later, Charlotte began teasing me about my apparent 'failure'. I'd not brought a girl back, and she saw it as a perfect opportunity to abuse me. She was so smug.

'Where's your lad then?' I asked, hitting back. 'If you've just had such an amazing date, where is he?'

Back and forth, back and forth we went, tearing into each other. Then we started throwing silly things at each other and the whole thing descended into stupidness and cruel name-calling.

I was only trying to stick up for myself but I admit I did throw some ham at her. It was a ridiculous thing to do, but it was the first thing that came to hand at the time.

Everyone separated us and I got told off for the ham incident. And for calling her a slag.

Then, while the lads were trying to calm me down, Charlotte came in and started the whole thing off again.

Scott grabbed me and took me outside.

'I hate him,' I could hear her screaming as I tried to shake off my own rage. 'Why is anyone friends with that man?'

She'd gone too far this time. And it was all because I had given her a silly little present to try and be nice. I was more than hacked off. I was fuming.

PARSNIP POINTERS

NO. 17: THINGS TO AVOID

Cheesy pick-up lines are always awful, even if you use them ironically. Girls hate them and won't take you seriously if you say them.

Never sneak up behind a girl and start dancing with her. It's creepy and a little bit threatening. You're more likely to get a slap in the face than a shag.

In fact, be careful about touching them at all if you don't know them. Being grabby is a total no-no.

Simple ways to touch a lass without being sleazy include holding her coat while she puts it on, offering her your hand on an uneven surface, catching her if she stumbles, and hugging or high-fiving her if she's pleased about something.

Name dropping is also a weak move on someone you hardly know. It might work on a few shallow girls, but generally as soon as you starting reeling off the network of celebs or club owners you know you're only making yourself look tacky.

Don't be too cocky or brag too much about yourself. Self-confidence is attractive, but too much of it is a huge turn-off.

CHAPTER 18

THE 'L' BOMB

The next day, Charlotte was sent home and I decided it was definitely for the best. Things were getting to boiling point between us and we needed to get away from each other. I felt free at last and tried to enjoy being unshackled.

But after I'd calmed down, I found that I actually missed her. When we went out soon after, to let off some steam, I wasn't in the mood to rampage through the town like I normally did. I was actually bored, and didn't even bother trying to pull.

I had entertainment in the form of Dan pulling a cougar and bringing her back to the house, but things felt so odd without Charlotte around and instead of feeling free I now felt like I wasn't myself anymore. I felt a bit deflated and I couldn't understand it.

Even Dan had pulled – where was Charlotte when I needed her? Why couldn't we just be shag buddies? Why did we have to go through so much hassle every time we hooked up?

She was back a few days later, full of remorse. I was glad to see her return and even happier when she apologised for what she'd done. But I knew it would still be for the best to keep my distance from her: I never wanted anything like that to happen again.

During her apology, she admitted she had been jealous, which was a first and I thought maybe it meant she had turned a corner. Only time would tell.

Later that morning, the phone rang and I wondered what job Anna had lined up for us next.

She said: 'Pack your bags, guys.'

'What, again?' I replied.

This time we were off to Barcelona. Or 'Barce-boner', as I declared it would be renamed once I'd finished with it. It was our best city destination yet and I couldn't wait to mingle with all the hot Spanish birds.

When we arrived, I had a heart-to-heart with Sophie, who always seemed to be able to see situations from both sides. Lying by the pool, she told me the bed sharing between me and Charlotte had to stop, and we needed to leave each other alone if we really wanted to properly move on. I knew she was right. I also knew that I had to be the strong one, because Charlotte was a lot weaker than me. She wanted a relationship and I didn't. I figured it was my responsibility to take charge of things.

I was glad I'd spoken to Sophie, but the conversation soon turned a little bit heavy, and I was glad when Dan dive-bombed the pool and interrupted us. It was the signal that it was time to party.

Barcelona was beautiful. It was autumn, so it wasn't exactly warm, but that didn't stop us having a good time. On the first day, Vicky and Charlotte had to take some lads on a sightseeing tour, so I decided to take the rest of the house on my own version of 'seeing the sights'.

We stopped off at a garage and picked up some little go-karts to drive around the city in. They were like Noddy cars and were hilarious. Scott, who is really tall, could hardly fit into his.

That night we hit the town hard. The girls went off on their own, so we decided to have a proper lads' night while they weren't around. Dan decided to take charge of our party schedule and we somehow ended up in a tranny bar. It was more than a little bit awkward.

It turned out that he'd asked someone in the street to recommend the best place to find some action, and whoever it was had obviously decided to have a laugh with him.

The entertainment started and we had no idea what to expect when the trannies came out and started giving us lap dances.

I decided to make the most of it and it was quite funny in the end. But we moved on after having our meal and met up with the girls to go to a proper club.

The next day I was sent with Dan and Holly to work a hen party, which was another great way of keeping my distance from Charlotte. It was pretty shit, though. There were girls and boys on the hen party, so it wasn't exactly easy pickings.

We got them trashed and made them do a bar crawl, which made the night a little better at least. But there was no pulling. When we got off work we met up with the rest of the house and went out drinking. But Charlotte was acting weird. Again. I tried to ignore it, but then she uttered those damning words: 'Gaz, can I have a word?'

I took a deep breath and went and sat down with her outside the bar. 'I feel like I'm totally spoiling your time here,' she said, very sadly. I could see she was deeply upset.

'We have a relationship and not one person can relate to what we're going through,' I said gently. 'We live together, we don't, we live together, we don't. It's a unique situation.'

She told me I didn't get how she felt, but I'm not made of stone. It was hurting me too.

'Do you think it was easy for me when you had a boyfriend?' I asked.

'You don't understand,' she said, starting to really sob. 'I love you. And I always have,' she added.

I hate seeing Charlotte cry. It always rips at my heart. She was pouring her feelings out and it stopped me in my tracks.

'I love you to bits, you know I do,' I told her.

'But not like that,' she wept, referring to my desire to stay single.

'No, it's not the same, no, but you know how much I love you,' I said. I wanted to finally make her understand my viewpoint, even though I knew it would hurt her to hear it.

'I want to know the truth,' she said bravely. 'Why did you lead us on? Why did you act like you did care about us? Why do you do the things you do?'

I literally didn't have the words to respond. I simply had no idea what to say and my silence must have meant more to her than anything I could have come out with if I had said anything. When she got up and walked away I knew that we were in big trouble. I was about to lose her friendship, which was the last thing I wanted. I felt deeply sad. It was a proper Barcelona breakdown.

So I went and chatted to the lads to try and deal with what

had just happened, but I felt shell-shocked and empty. I guess in hindsight this moment had always been inevitable, but back then I honestly hadn't seen it coming.

The next day there was an awful atmosphere in the house, so we all went down to the beach for a change of scene. I respected Charlotte's honesty, but I couldn't lie to her. We just didn't have a future together.

Normally, when a girl drops the L-bomb and you don't feel the same way, you can sack them off – at least for a while. It might seem like a cold thing to do at the time, but after something as big as a love declaration it's always better to have some time and space before you see each other again. But I couldn't. I had to see and experience her suffering every single day.

We flew back to Newcastle, and I still had no idea what the next step should be. I was stuck in the *Geordie Shore* house with someone who I cared about but continually kept hurting. This was my job – people expected me to pull girls and party hard on screen. But real feelings were colliding with the near fantasy world we'd all created. I didn't want to upset anyone.

My head was a total mess.

James decided that we needed to do something completely different – have a bit of group bonding – so he took us all to an outdoor bootcamp to get some exercise. We were all so out of shape from all the drinking and partying we were doing on the show that maybe some natural endorphins would cheer us up?

The girls hated having to run around so much, but I loved every second of it. Focusing on something other than my emotions was such a relief. I felt really refreshed once it was over.

GAZ (AND MY PARSNIP)

When we got back, there was more bad news for everyone – Ricci and Vicky had finally agreed to break up. And there was more: Ricci had decided to leave *Geordie Shore* to give Vicky the space they both needed.

They'd been arguing like mad all month and Ricci had even left the house for a while at one point to try and save the relationship. But he and Vicky both knew that they would only keep arguing if they stayed in the house together.

It was sad, but we all thought it was the best thing to do. We decided to give Ricci one final big send off: a proper lads' night out on the Toon.

I felt that it was only right that we all got totally smashed to mark the occasion. Dan went off with the cougar again, after he spotted her in the club, then I pulled a worldie and left Ricci and Scott to knock back some more booze together.

I knew that's what Ricci would have wanted us to do.

At the end of the night, Scott put Ricci in a taxi to take him back to his own home and we went back to the *Geordie Shore* house without him. It was time for everyone to move on.

The girls called a family meeting and announced that they wanted to have a house party to cheer themselves up. It was a fair enough plan.

'We want it to be American-themed fancy dress,' they told us, laughing. I loved dressing up. It was going to be mint.

Sophie asked her boyfriend Joel to DJ, and we all got busy preparing for the party. The girls went to the fancy dress store without the lads and actually chose our outfits for us, so I knew I'd end up having to wear something awful.

But we needed to make idiots of ourselves to lighten the mood, so I wasn't bothered what they chose for me.

I ended up dressed as a big blue Smurf.

THE 'L' BOMB

It was an inspired choice, but it did mean there was one problem: it would be impossible to discreetly pull anyone, because they'd end up with incriminating blue make-up all over them once we'd finished!

As the party got under way, a tidal wave of girls streamed through the door, all dressed in teeny tiny hot pants and not much else.

Where were all the lads?

It may sound like it was great for us to have loads of lasses to choose from. But with no lads to pull, the girls were not going to be happy.

Charlotte was really upset. She had dressed as Gene Simmons, the lead singer of the rock band Kiss, so she was, in fact, dressed as a bloke.

She looked great, but she was no competition for the stream of sexy cowgirls who were lassoing our attentions.

Throughout the night, I was either aware of her watching me, or else felt as if her eyes were burning into the back of my head. The party was not going well.

I decided to take a girl upstairs and give her a tour of the house, but Charlotte followed us and gave me a right earful.

I was shocked by the real venom I could see in her eyes. I'd never seen her like that. Seeing me with a girl had tipped her over the edge and I didn't know how we'd ever come back from it.

It's fair to say that from then on the party was ruined.

The next morning, Anna called and was absolutely furious about what had happened. Charlotte knew that what she'd done was wrong, but she couldn't take it back now. She was told to pack her bags and leave the house.

Everyone was gutted it had come to such a dramatic head.

But if Charlotte and me continued to live under the same roof it was possible we'd end up seriously harming each other.

I stayed in bed while she packed, not wanting to face her. Everyone wished her well as they put her into a taxi, but still I didn't emerge from my room. There was nothing left to say.

She actually hated me. And now, so did the rest of the girls.

What was I meant to do at the party – lock myself in a cupboard? There were 40 girls and five lads – I couldn't have not talked to a lass.

But the girls were behaving like they wanted to string me up and chop my parsnip off. Luckily we had something to distract us – we were told we were off again, and this time we were going to the French Alps.

I knew that it would be weird without Charlotte. On all the trips we'd made so far, me and Charlotte had done something to make the mini-breaks memorable.

In Amsterdam we'd kind of got back together, in Prague she'd looked after me when I was sick, in Barcelona she'd told me she loved me... Now I was going skiing without her.

We had to make the most of our final trip away. And most importantly we had to try and repair the divide that had split the house, yet again, into girls vs boys. I didn't really feel like partying and pulling. I was consumed by guilt.

Arriving in the Alps, we couldn't believe we'd finally found somewhere colder than Newcastle. There was deep snow everywhere and we knew that the girls we'd meet would be posh university student types, who would definitely like the bit of rough we could offer.

I still wasn't feeling 100 per cent, but Scott wasn't having any of my wallowing and took us out for après-ski drinks almost instantly.

THE 'L' BOMB

At the bar, I could tell everyone was missing Charlotte. I was missing her too, but I knew we needed to make the best of a bad situation. And if this trip was going to be any kind of success, I needed Vicky on my side.

Over a round of drinks, I told her: 'I don't want my and Charlotte's thing to affect everyone on this trip.'

We had a long chat and eventually we decided to call a truce and let bygones be bygones while we were away. Things got better after that and we actually had a good night out in the end. The girls and the boys all got drunk together and we surprised ourselves by having fun, despite the situation.

Watching the girls tottering around in the snow in their heels was hilarious. We were all mortal drunk. Maybe it was the altitude...

Joel arrived the next day and when me and the lads were told we had a hen party to look after I had an idea – we'd take him with us and see if he could finally prove himself to be a decent lad who loved Sophie.

We arrived at the bar crawl and the place was chock full of posh fanny. We waded in and got them all smashed, taking them from bar to bar in the sub-zero temperatures.

Shockingly, Joel was actually behaving himself, so we got him eyeballing shots to try and get him really drunk to see if that would change things. But despite our best efforts, he continued to be a good lad. We even had a laugh with him. Maybe we were finally bonding.

Scott and Dan pulled almost instantly, but although I'd got chatting to a hot blonde, I couldn't bring myself to close the deal. It didn't feel right without Charlotte there.

I went back to the house alone, where we picked everyone else up and went straight back out to party.

Everyone was finally getting on again and it felt amazing.

The Alps was definitely doing us the world of good.

Back home in Newcastle, as filming drew to a close, we organised one last night out to say goodbye to each other. I called Ricci and invited him along and he agreed to join us. But when the girls called Charlotte to ask her if she would come too, she said no.

She actually said she never wanted to see me again, which obviously hurt a bit. I hoped that she just needed more time to clear her head.

On our last night, we wanted to go out with a bang. Ricci arrived and it was so good to see him. We all danced and had a wicked time. I was glad we were leaving on good terms with each other, even though I was still worried about what would happen with Charlotte.

We had designated it a family night, so none of the lads took any notice of the random girls they'd normally be trying to pull. And we went home in the early hours, on a high from our successful night out.

The next day, it was time to pack our bags and say goodbye once more. It had been yet another explosive month in the house and we were still feeling the shock of it all.

Anna arrived, which was unusual for the end of the season. She didn't look happy, and the look on her face was one we sadly recognised.

'I'll be in touch about the future,' she told us. 'Next time there are going to be some big changes.'

We had no idea what she meant, but it was yet more confirmation that I needed to sort out my life outside the house. I needed to get my finances organised and plan for the future.

This kind of life couldn't last forever. Nothing ever does.

Saying goodbye, I felt that familiar feeling of sadness and relief.

It would be good for us all to get away and clear our heads once more, but I was still worried about the Charlotte situation. I decided to go and see how she was, and to try to cheer her up by giving her our 'house' goldfish, who were named Scrambled, Egg and Toast.

These fish belonged to all of us in a way, they were our 'collective' pets, but she loved the little creatures more than anyone and I knew she would definitely be missing them. I hoped that she would see it as a peace offering.

It felt a bit mad, driving along with a bowl of fish next to me. But nothing on *Geordie Shore* was normal.

When I arrived at Charlotte's house, I didn't know what to expect. Would she answer the door and punch me in the mouth?

Or take the fish and slam the door in my face?

At least I was trying to make amends – for everyone, not just for myself. I truly wanted her to come back. I knew that having her in the house would always make my life more difficult than it needed to be, but I would miss her so much if she wasn't there next time. It wouldn't be the same without her and she needed to know that.

When there was no answer at the door, I put the fish on her doorstep and left. On the way back I got a text from her, saying she needed time to get her head together.

Maybe there was hope yet.

Back at home, I took my mind off things by working flat out on my new business venture. I still travelled up and down the country doing personal appearances at nightclubs, but every bit of the little spare time I had was spent getting the shop ready.

This was my master plan. I needed to get myself financially secure for the future, and having a business was the way forward. I never wanted to run out of money. Ever. And I was happy to work hard to make sure it never happened.

On Project 722's opening day, which took place in November 2012, the store was absolutely jam-packed. Word had got out that I was making a personal appearance there, and the queues snaked right through the Metro Centre.

Debenhams even complained because the queue was so long it was blocking their entrance. I felt I deserved it. For the past year I had worked harder than I ever had in my life and now this business was going to work hard for me.

As I've said, people may think that I spend my time drinking and banging birds, and that's true. But it's not the only thing I do. Although people who have to do hard physical jobs all day, or even jobs they hate, may not see what I do as work at all. So even though it's not work in the way most people see it, what I do does require a lot of thought, energy, effort and tact, and it isn't always easy. I work a lot harder than people think I do.

I'm constantly promoting something, or posing for photos, or travelling to an event to make sure the people there have an extra-special time – I'm selling myself practically 24 hours a day, and I take it very seriously.

I can't ever be grumpy, or boring. I have to always be happy and friendly, even if I feel like crap. I think it's very important to respect people and I would never turn anyone away if they came up to me for a chat. I'm not moaning. On the contrary, I'm always saying how much I love my life.

But it's not all fun and games – no one's life is, no matter how perfect it may seem to people on the outside. And there is much more to me than meets the eye, just like there is with everyone you meet. We're all much more than just one-dimensional beings.

Shortly before Christmas, as I was still buzzing with the excitement of the new shop, I smashed my six-figure target. I splashed out and treated my family and friends, before quickly setting myself a new challenge – to make triple that in the next year. I knew that with Billy, Shaq and Kay by my side I could do it. We were a dream team, a family, and we would all succeed together.

Having something to aim for really motivated me. I had finally figured out that my desire to be the best could actually really work for me. And I didn't always need to compete with anyone else to gain satisfaction. By setting my own outrageous targets and challenges, I only had myself to beat, and it made me work harder than ever. I was on fire and once again Christmas was a good time for the Beadle household.

In January 2013, me and Shaq flew to Australia for our first solo tour down under. I was the first cast member to book venues overseas, and I was constantly trying to think 'outside of the box' to make myself as successful as possible.

I knew that the show was doing well in Australia, and I remembered how good it had been when me and Charlotte had gone on a promo tour there, nearly a year earlier. And that was before the show had even really aired in Oz.

Twelve months and five seasons later everyone knew who I was and wanted to party with me. We were booked solid for the whole month we were out there, and had a relentless travelling schedule organised just to fit everything in.

GAZ (AND MY PARSNIP)

It was an unreal experience – much more overwhelming than I could ever have imagined. Walking out in front of thousands of people, all screaming my name – I was blown away. I couldn't believe I was famous so many miles away from Newcastle.

When I'd started on *Geordie Shore*, I figured a few people might recognise me walking down the streets back home, but I had no idea my life would change so drastically. I never expected the show to become such a hit, I never expected it to carry on for so many seasons, and I never expected to get so emotionally attached to all my fellow cast members.

I had a dream life. Travelling all over the world, being treated like royalty, getting paid a fortune: never in my wildest dreams had I expected things to turn out the way they had.

In February, I flew back home and continued to work my way around the country, making countless personal appearances in front of our fans.

As spring arrived, the shop was doing well and I was bang on target to reach my next financial milestone.

When MTV got in touch and told us where Series Six would take place I couldn't believe it.

I was going back to Australia.

NO. 18: THE DAYLIGHT PULL

You don't have to be in a bar or a club to get lucky with a lass – you can line up a future shag even while you're doing something as mundane as shopping.

There are many ways of going about a daylight pull. Asking girls for directions is always a good opener. Or you can be direct and say something like: 'I'm sorry to bother you, but I knew if I didn't say hi I'd kick myself all day...'

Asking them for advice is a good option if you're in a shopping centre alone. Say you're looking for a certain kind of gift for a sister or female friend and ask if they have any suggestions.

To move things on, you need to find common ground by asking her what she likes to do. If she enjoys clubbing for example, you could say you're going to an awesome club at the weekend and would love it if she brought along some mates.

It's a no-pressure invite and doesn't make you sound too keen.

If you're getting along really well, then you can choose to go in for the 'instant date' move. Girls love spontaneity because they think it's romantic when guys do spur-of-the-moment things. Say something like: 'I'm meeting my mates later, do you fancy grabbing a coffee first?'

This shows that you're popular and busy, but also suggests you must really like her if you want to keep chatting to her so much.

CHAPTER 19

THE SHORE GOES DOWN UNDER

As I boarded the plane for my second 24-hour journey that year, I was ridiculously excited. I knew that we were all going to have an amazing time together, and I would get to explore the country much more than when I'd been there earlier that year.

I arrived in Sydney and made my way to meet the others at our Australian pad, which I quickly discovered was missing Charlotte, Scott, Dan and Ricci. Charlotte and Scott would be coming later, and apparently Charlotte was loved up with another boyfriend. But Ricci wasn't coming to Oz at all.

We'd all miss him being around, but I hoped that with him gone, Vicky could have a good time and we wouldn't have so many arguments.

Dan was gone too, having decided to move on from the show.

I hoped that maybe things would be okay now between me and Charlotte. If she was off limits I reckoned I could get on with pulling birds and she would have to leave me alone. But when she'd had a boyfriend before it hadn't changed things, so I wasn't going to get my hopes up just yet.

Me, Holly, Sophie and James had just about caught up with each other and explored our new pad, when suddenly we heard a roaring sound coming from outside.

We looked out of the window and saw a guy on a monster of a motorbike, heading our way. It was our new boss, Steve the Shearer.

He strode into the house wearing a cowboy hat and shades, looking like Crocodile Dundee gone horribly wrong. And he made it clear he was determined to take us in hand from the very beginning. He was a no nonsense, down-to-earth, hard-working kind of guy and I knew he would be a lot firmer than Anna, Sam, or even the much-hated Cancun Chris.

We always forget that we're there to supposedly work, because all we really want to do is party. But before he left, Steve made it clear that he was going to make us remember our duties – and keep reminding us of them.

Scott arrived, and with my wingman beside me, we all went out for our first night on the town. I wasted no time in getting a girl to come back to our Sydney gaff.

That night I christened the shag pad with her and was so glad that Charlotte wasn't there to see it. It was only our first night and I'd got laid. I hoped it was a sign of things to come.

The next night, we all went out on the town again. Holly and James had some kind of meltdown in the club and while me and Scott were busy trying to pull, all I could hear was her screaming at the top of her voice.

I had no idea what had happened, but I watched as she was unceremoniously kicked out of the club.

We'd only been there 10 minutes!

For once, it wasn't me involved in all the drama. My plan was to get a bird and skulk off with her back home. And that's exactly what I did.

Since I'd had the shag pad the night before, it was Scott's turn to have it, which posed a bit of a dilemma. I couldn't take her back to my room, because Vicky was in it. So I turfed James out and shagged her in his room – on what would actually be Charlotte's bed, if she ever arrived.

This was something I only realised when I was halfway through doing the deed. Oops. I could only hope she never found out.

The next day, after I'd waved off my lass, I heard a familiar screeching sound coming from the hallway – Charlotte had arrived. She was civil to me, and hugged me hello, but I could tell she was making an effort to keep her distance from me.

She was in a good mood and was on top form all day. The atmosphere was surprisingly fine between us and I was relieved.

I hoped it would last.

Our job in Sydney was to entertain people on party buses, which was something we knew we could definitely do well. The lasses in Oz were really fit too, which helped. On the beaches, they were always bouncing around in bikinis playing volleyball, and it was easy to get involved in a game.

Australia was going to be amazing.

But before we could get well and truly stuck in – to work and play – we had another surprise visitor: Jay was back.

When he walked through the door we couldn't believe it was him. It was one of the best moments I can remember on the show. As soon as we saw his cheeky face we all jumped on him. I was genuinely so happy to see him.

After so much tension ramping up in our past few seasons of filming, we all hoped that having Jay back would change things. He had been the daddy of the house. Daddy could sort us all out if we started fighting again.

We learned that he wouldn't be there for the whole stint – he'd only come to visit us for a while. But any time with him there would be great, and I think we even sneakily hoped we could convince him to stay longer.

Over the next week or so, our schedules were jam-packed. We went kayaking, we went to a safari park, we learnt how to surf, we went sky-diving... We had one amazing experience after another.

Scott was getting more and more competitive with me, and I was definitely up for the challenge of beating him – whether it was to be at pulling birds or any of the physical things we had to do. It made it a little bit more exciting to have someone to beat. The girls thought it was a bit pathetic, but I didn't care. They thought he was trying to challenge my 'King of the Lads' title, but I just saw it as a bit of harmless fun between friends.

If I pulled, Scott would panic and wander around like a headless chicken trying to stay level with me. And if I saw him kissing someone, it spurred me on to find a girl sharpish, so I wasn't left out. It kept us both on our toes and made our nights out very interesting.

One night, Holly was using the shag pad, so he had to use the sofa to bang the girl he'd brought back. But he didn't realise that Charlotte had got mortal and pissed herself on the cushions before he got going. When I found out I nearly wet myself too, I was laughing so much.

Before Jay left we did our best to beg him to stay. It had

been such a breath of fresh air to have him there – no one had fought, everyone had been happy and relaxed – no one wanted him to go. But despite our protests, he flew back to the UK and left us all to it.

James really felt his absence the most. He was feeling left out because he had a girlfriend back home and so he couldn't join in on the pulling that me and Scott were doing.

With Jay there, he'd had someone to chat to while we were off banging birds. But now he was gone he would be alone again.

I felt sorry for him but I wasn't going to stop having fun just because his balls were in a girlfriend-shaped vice.

And I noticed that Charlotte began behaving completely differently as well. She was much more subdued than usual, and I discovered it was because she was missing her new boyfriend, Mitch. She was cool and calm towards me and I took baby steps to try and reignite our friendship. I didn't want things to go back to how they were when we were fighting, but I did want to be friends. It was weird and awkward, but at least we were speaking.

Almost as soon as Jay was gone, the arguments started again. Firstly, it was the girls who kicked off at each other. Vicky had gone out on a date and rejoined the rest of the girls at a club only to find Charlotte absolutely mortal. Something was bound to go wrong and true to *Geordie Shore* form, it quickly did.

Charlotte told them she'd found things tense with the girls since she'd arrived and Vicky wasn't impressed. 'Are you taking the piss?' she said, and told her she'd changed since she'd been in Oz, and not for the better.

They glared at each other and it was obvious that battle

sides were being drawn. It was Charlotte and Holly vs Sophie and Vicky. It looked like World War Three was brewing and us lads tried to stay out of it.

It was odd watching the girls argue, like a real blast from the past. They hadn't fallen out like this for months and always for the most part got on well with each other, unless a new girl was involved.

It was Charlotte who got kicked out of the club this time.

In the morning, the girls felt sorry that they'd fallen out and made up pretty quickly. But it wasn't long before the house was at war again.

And who was next in the firing line?

Me.

The competition between me and Scott had started to really hot up under the strong Australian sun. It was supposed to be a bit of fun, but we were constantly trying to outdo each other in the pulling stakes, and it soon began to wind everyone up.

We were bringing different girls back all the time, even on family nights, and it wasn't long before the girls and James got sick of it.

Were we being childish? Maybe.

Did it matter? No.

Winning was all that mattered.

We weren't doing anything wrong. We were both single and just having a good time. But for some reason it was making everyone very angry.

The girls got territorial and clubbed together like a pack of wolves to confront us. Together, they told us off for treating the house like a shagging hotel. We backed into a corner, while the girls screamed at us to grow up and have some respect.

'We're single lads!' I said. 'What do you want us to do?'

Fingers were being pointed, people were yelling – and bizarrely it was all directed at me.

It became very clear that it was me they were annoyed at, not Scott, even though we were both as bad as each other. James sided with the girls – all because he was feeling left out.

He was acting like a big girl, that's for sure.

Scott and I decided to leave the house for a bit.

I could almost hear Charlotte's pleasure that everyone was finally having a go at me and it was infuriating. I wasn't doing anything wrong. Why was I being treated like this, I wondered?

Everyone hated me, apart from Scott.

We both left, fuming with anger and hurt, and went and stayed in a hotel to cool off. When we arrived back at the house, we didn't know what to expect. Everyone was playing bowls together outside and when we tentatively walked over we could see they weren't in a forgiving mood.

Scott started chatting to them right away, trying to make peace, but I just skulked around, waiting for someone to say something.

Awkward…

Vicky explained that they were mad because they wanted us to all have fun together, but because me and Scott were so intent on beating each other, we always ended up leaving them when we were out. So they were just upset because they wanted the gang to play together, and not run off with the other kids. It was like being back in a school playground again. I could kind of see their point. We did spend most of our time going off on our own little pulling missions and leaving them to their own devices.

'Okay,' I thought. 'I can fix this.'

I stepped in and offered up a solution – on family nights

we'd call a truce to our pulling competition, and only be with them.

We'd limit ourselves to two shagging nights a week. Would that make them happy?

But they weren't overly impressed, so I just apologised, to try and move things on for the sake of the 'gang'.

It wasn't perfect, but it was better than not speaking.

We went out with Vicky and Holly to try and have a good time and I actually had a laugh with Vicky for the first time in ages. I'd forgotten how much fun she could be.

There was no pulling that night – well at least not with girls outside of the gang. So Scott got around the rule of the night by flirting like mad with Holly.

Technically, he wasn't doing anything wrong. And it meant he was still beating me. It was a surprising move, and one which I couldn't counter. I certainly wasn't going to try it on with Vicky!

When we got back, me and Vicky carried on chatting, while Holly and Scott got it on in his bed.

We left them to it. I knew he'd regret it in the morning and I'd have the last laugh then. Holly quite liked him, and if he messed around with her and then pulled other lasses on another night he'd be in serious trouble. She would turn into his Charlotte.

Things seemed better when we all woke up, and with Vicky now firmly on my side I felt I had another ally in the house.

Do you know what? I hated being the focus of all that rage.

I started to get on better with James and things even improved with Charlotte, who finally started to chat to me again. We had a proper family night and I had a good time with everyone, at last.

THE SHORE GOES DOWN UNDER

For once no one was yelling at each other. It obviously couldn't last – it never did in our mad family – but while it did I was determined to entertain everyone. Later that night I ran naked, with my willy tucked between my legs, and jumped into the pool. Everyone laughed and we were back on an even keel.

But I wasn't going to be a nun for the rest of my time in Oz. So a few nights later I went out on the pull, and brought three girls back to the house – accidentally including a girl that Scott had shagged before.

Scott wasn't impressed, and wasted no time in confronting me about it. He started to have a go at me while I was rummaging around in the fridge, getting some drinks for my conquests.

'Would I ever do that to you?' he asked, suddenly flanked by James for support.

I didn't want an argument and told him to lay off. It wasn't even my fault she was there. I was only really interested in one of them, but she'd only agreed to come back if she could bring her mates – including Scott's former shag. I was determined not to get cockblocked by Scott, so I walked away.

But in the end it wasn't long before all three girls were in my bed, and it was looking like I was going to have a foursome. Screw Scott – who would turn that down?

I was definitely winning the battle of the alpha males.

Soon after, Sophie's boyfriend Joel turned up, which made her very happy – but this event didn't please everyone. He announced his arrival by banging a load of pots and pans together to wake us up. *Ouch*.

Holly and Charlotte knew that they wouldn't have Sophie all to themselves anymore, which they weren't pleased about.

But hopefully lonely James would spend time with him, while me and Scott could get on with our competition and the girls could have some Sophie time. It could work out perfectly...

One night Scott proudly announced that he'd shagged one more bird than me so far. I wasn't bothered. I liked an added incentive and if he wanted a war, he could have one. 'Let the games really begin,' I said, clasping his hand in mine and giving him a grin.

I would take it all in good grace if I lost, but I knew he'd be mad if he didn't win.

Scott had pulled ahead in an early lead, but there was a long way to go yet, so I let him be smug about it. Mam had taught me about taking defeat gracefully and I knew how to behave respectfully with my competitors.

But obviously Scott's mam hadn't taught him in quite the same way, because when I soon started to overtake him, his jealously was pretty plain to see.

We were out clubbing one night when he came over and started an argument with me – I knew why he was annoyed, although he was behaving like a right tit about it.

He had pulled a lass, while I had three birds all to myself, which meant I was definitely winning. He couldn't handle it, and even said he was never going to speak to me again.

It was so stupid it was almost funny. I couldn't believe we were actually falling out over it. Back at the house, I had brought the three girls back, while he'd brought the one lass with him. I needed a whole room to myself to satisfy all of them, so I told Scott he'd have to shag his bird on the sofa.

He'd challenged my alpha male crown, and I was making sure he knew he'd never have it. He actually had hatred in his eyes when I told him to use the sofa. But I had a foursome to get on with and I took no notice of his petty drunken jealousy.

He had to man up if he wanted to challenge me. But instead he decided to take his anger out on some of the objects in the house. Smart move. Not.

Soon after, I went into the famous 'Australian Outback' with Charlotte, Vicky and Holly. We ate round a campfire, melted marshmallows on sticks and just had a low-key relaxing time together. It was nice to have a break from all the partying and chill out for a bit.

I chatted with Vicky and told her I knew that my friendship with Scott was more important than our stupid competition. But it was him who was fuelling it, and I wasn't going to back down if he wanted to really challenge me to some kind of silly duel.

Vicky admitted that his attitude was annoying everyone.

In the outback we learned how to shear sheep, which turned out to be tremendously funny. We had to hold them down and give them a full-on shave. The shearing room stank, the sheep kept shitting themselves, and the girls were squealing. It was certainly an experience.

When we got back to Sydney, the girls decided to cockblock Scott's next pulling efforts, and I certainly wasn't going to stop them. They'd also put him on a drinking ban, to try and get him to calm down. It was going to be an interesting first night back.

And when Scott started getting friendly with a girl in a club, they crowded round her, all smiles and sweet words, and began dancing with her.

Scott thought they were just being nice – it was so funny to watch him with this big grin on his face, completely oblivious to the fact that the girls were making sure that he was going to go home alone that night.

He was crestfallen when he figured it out.

Soon after, we were told that a counsellor would be coming to give us a group therapy session. We thought it would be hilarious.

When the appointed time came, in walked our counsellor. She was a tiny slip of a woman, who wanted us to tell her what had got us all so riled up during our time in Australia.

If we kicked off, there was no way she could pull us apart. I nearly suggested she come back another time – with bodyguards!

We were all pretty calm and blasé about it in the beginning, but once everyone started airing their grievances, blood pressures really began to rise. I think it actually made everyone angrier than they'd been before she walked in.

Holly raged at Scott, Sophie raged at Joel, Charlotte revealed she was glad that her and I were no longer close – it was torture.

I kept my mouth shut as she spewed out her hatred of me, revealing everything she disliked about me. But I was really pissed off when she said that sometimes the sex between us was boring.

Boring? It wasn't true, for one, and secondly, I had a reputation to protect. What was she doing?

Scott was loving it, but I was squirming like the sheep we'd sheared only days before. I was so glad when the session ended, but it had made it obvious that me and Charlotte needed to talk.

I'd thought things were okay between us, but she was obviously still upset.

THE SHORE GOES DOWN UNDER

So I took her to the beach and tried to be honest with her.

It was so hard to believe that only a year ago we'd been so close. In our first ever month in the house we'd got on so well, and I missed the nights we'd lie awake just chatting and making each other laugh. Things had got so twisted since then.

Those first few weeks together were some of the fondest memories of my time on the show so far. But they were being tainted by our current situation. And I knew I was partly to blame.

'I did play with your emotions,' I admitted. 'I can't even blame it on the drink, I did sometimes sleep with you when I knew I shouldn't. I did bang girls when I knew you wouldn't like it.'

I hadn't meant to hurt her, but I had and it was time for me to man up. Charlotte had been waiting for my apology for months, but even though I had now said I was sorry, it was too late.

'You've lost us,' she said. 'We'll never be friends again.'

I had to settle for civility, and hope that she could eventually forgive me. 'I'm pleased we can talk to each other,' I said. 'I'd rather just be civil than not talk to you, ever.'

I had to suck it up if we were ever going to repair our broken friendship.

On Scott's birthday, we all went out to a club and agreed not to pull so that we could have a good time together as a family.

Sophie and Joel got absolutely mortal and decided to give us all a little bit of a live sex show in the club. Even I was shocked at how far they took it. They were practically shagging in front of us.

Scott had a brilliant time and I think everyone was surprised that we stuck to our plan not to shag. We all went home without shag partners, and decided to dress Scott up in a gimp outfit and handcuff him to the piano. It was a very funny moment.

When me and Charlotte had to work together on the party bus soon after, I'll admit I was nervous about it. Now that I knew how she really felt it would test our new truce to the limit.

But she surprised me. Somehow in the outback she had found a kind of peace with everything, and she spent the whole night being the best wingwoman I could hope for. She actually lined up the girls who wanted to pull me. It was odd, but I definitely felt more at ease about things with her. I thought we could build on it to get our friendship back.

After that, it was off to Newcastle for the gang – Newcastle Australia, that is. We couldn't wait to see what the Oz version of our favourite city was like.

At first things seemed relaxed in the new city.

It was warm, the beaches were beautiful, and they even had fish and chips – minus the mushy peas and curry sauce, sadly.

But on the very first night Charlotte started sulking because she didn't want to go out. We left her at home to calm down and went clubbing, where I pulled two birds and Scott pulled one.

Holly wasn't impressed. And neither was Vicky. Luckily their anger was mainly directed at Scott, who they felt was getting away with bad behaviour all the time, while everyone else got punished. When we all arrived home, birds in tow, with a big box of pizza, Holly kicked off, big time.

She huddled with the girls, moaning about the situation. We

were downstairs with the birds we wanted to bang, and all we could hear was bitching from the girls' bedroom.

It was a proper cockblocking attempt but we weren't going to let it stop us. I gave Holly, Vicky and Charlotte some pizza and put them to bed as if they were children.

Then I pushed two beds together and got it on with the girls I'd brought back while Scott commandeered the sofa for his sexual gymnastics.

The next day, Charlotte, Holly and Scott all got kicked out for their recent displays of anger. So Holly got what she wanted even though she got caught in the crossfire.

They stayed in the 'punishment hotel', where we were sent when we'd got into trouble in the house, while the rest of us went to the most haunted house in Australia to spend the night.

Located in the town of Junee in New South Wales, the Monte Cristo Homestead was first built by a local pioneer in 1885 and was apparently now home to a number of terrifying ghosts.

While staying the night in the Victorian manor house, we were told to expect phantom sounds, strange lights and even ghostly apparitions. Loads of people had apparently tragically died there, including a child who was dropped down the stairs, a maid who fell from the balcony and a stable boy who was burnt to death.

Sophie was terrified and kept seeing things. But luckily Vicky was rational and calmed her down.

The night passed fairly uneventfully really. The ghosts weren't going to mess with us proper Geordies. Sophie was the scariest thing in there to be honest.

Newcastle back home was our own personal playground –

birds, booze and the best nightlife. But Newcastle Oz did have its plus points.

The beaches were ever so slightly better than Whitley Bay, and you could go sand surfing and riding through the desert on sand buggies. I love the Toon, but Australia had some of the most amazing landscapes and fun things to do.

Back in Sydney, we all went dolphin watching. I knew I'd like the dolphins because apart from humans it's said that they're the only animals that have sex for pleasure. They were the 'Gazs of the sea' and I felt we were kindred spirits.

Charlotte and I actually had a lovely moment on the boat as the waves crashed around us – she confided in me that she was worried about what it would be like to see her boyfriend Mitch again after spending so much time apart.

I gave her some advice, and kept it as friendly as possible. I still felt like I was treading on eggshells, but finally having her open up to me felt good.

When we got back from the dolphin watching, we found out that Holly and Scott were back too and I hoped things could get back to normal.

We went out to a themed club and the Scott vs Gaz competition quickly started up again. The girls, once more, were not impressed. Why couldn't they leave us alone and get on with their own lives?

At the end of the night, Vicky wanted me to go to a pie shop with her to get food for everyone. But I was a bit pissed and I saw it as a dig at my failure to pull that night. This was because it seemed that you only went to the pie shop if you'd not managed to get a girl to come back with you that night. It felt like she was rubbing it in.

Suddenly we were arguing, but I knew it wasn't a real barny

– we'd be absolutely fine once we got home and started to sober up. It was just a drunken tiff. I even said sorry to Vicky in the car and she quickly accepted my apology. The whole thing had been nonsense and we both knew it.

But when we got back, James decided to get involved, and tried to goad me into an argument. He had a girlfriend, so he wasn't out on the pull like me and Scott and he was still feeling left out.

He'd been spending all his time with the girls, but he didn't have to. We weren't leaving him out, we just had different agendas in Australia. Just because he wasn't pulling, he didn't want any of the lads to pull either. He'd been waiting for an opportunity to take his anger out on me about it and now he felt he had one.

He came to find me, angling for a war of words. But I stayed in my room, trying to avoid an altercation. I could hear him slagging me off, and I was getting madder and madder. I tried my absolute hardest to stay away from him, but he pushed his way into my room and I could see there was no avoiding a bust-up.

This wasn't a fight about Vicky – this was much more deep-rooted than that. It was pointless. Why had he got so wound up? He said he was defending Vicky, but me and Vicky were fine.

He had his own agenda and issues and needed to deal with them. We used to be mates. I couldn't believe the hatred that I saw in his eyes.

Everyone said they were trying to keep the family together, but it felt like they were just trying to control each other. It was pathetic. And the next day he got kicked out, just like he deserved to be.

GAZ (AND MY PARSNIP)

Things were better with him gone. But without me knowing, Charlotte and Sophie were telling tales on me to Steve – saying that the fight between me and James was my fault too. For some reason they were trying to get me kicked out as well.

I took the singles on an amazing boat trip, and Charlotte, Sophie and Joel went shark diving. We were having incredible experiences, and making the most of the little time we had left in Oz.

But thanks to Charlotte and Sophie telling on me, Steve decided to chuck me out of the house too! Which meant I had to spend my last few days down under with James. Steve told me I had to apologise to him as well. Whatever. There was no way I was doing that. He'd ruined my remaining time in Australia. He could sing for his apology.

I made my way to the punishment hotel.

When we were alone, neither James nor I knew what to say, so we just stood silently next to each other, waiting for the other to say something. I wanted an apology but he was being stubborn. It was far too soon to resolve our differences. I was glad that at least we had separate rooms. While everyone was out clubbing, we were stuck in the hotel together. It was shit.

The next day, feeling very sorry for myself, I went back to the house and packed my things up. But Charlotte wasn't there, so I couldn't even say goodbye to her.

I never thought that my time in Australia would end like this – not speaking to James and not saying bye to Charlotte.

So I wrote her a letter, apologising for everything, and left it on her bed. Then I went back to spend my last night at the punishment hotel, before flying back to the UK the next day. I was gutted.

I felt defeated by it all. I apologised to James for winding him up, even though I didn't think I should be the one to do it. But things had gone too far and someone needed to put an end to it. He immediately said sorry to me in return and, like deflated balloons, we both went to bed early in the punishment hotel.

The next day, back at the house, everyone left to go to the airport one by one. At the hotel, I started to panic about Charlotte. I couldn't let her leave without saying goodbye: the letter wasn't enough to express how I truly felt. So I raced back to speak to her face to face before I left.

It was a hard conversation. But I wanted to square things with her. I wished her well with Mitch and told her he was a lucky lad. I felt much better for it, and I hoped she would too.

It was a long flight back home.

Especially when I discovered that Scott had actually taken my shagging crown on the last night – while I was locked up with James. He only beat me by one or two girls overall, but a win was a win.

I was no longer the king of the shaggers. I took it in good grace.

PARSNIP POINTERS

NO. 19: PULLING A STRIPPER

They're super hot, they've got it all on show, they're great dancers and they give you their full and undivided attention no matter what you look like – no wonder all blokes fantasise about pulling strippers.

But it doesn't have to be just a fantasy. Here's how...

Okay, so at first you have to accept that they are going to see you as just a business transaction. They've seen hundreds of guys drooling in front of them, all just like you. So you have to make yourself stand out if you're going to have a chance at pulling one.

Let her know you're not just a regular pervy punter by saying that your mates have dragged you to the club that night.

Take control of the conversation. Most strippers didn't originally dream of shedding their clothes for cash and many would rather be models or actresses, or are only doing it to support themselves while they're studying at university, or bringing up children alone.

Get her to open up to you by asking about her ambitions. Ask her what she's working towards, what her goals are. This way you're talking to the girl, cutting past the professional stripper act she's putting on.

Don't turn into a gibbering wreck, even though everything she's doing is designed to turn you on and make you go weak at the knees. Stay confident and try and flirt back with her to show her you can handle a little teasing.

THE SHORE GOES DOWN UNDER

Then write your number on a napkin and walk away.
Hopefully your phone will ring as soon as her shift is over.

CHAPTER 20

EXPLOSIONS AND SHOCKS

When we got back to the UK, spring was ending and summer was just beginning. I briefly caught up with my family, and hurriedly planned my schedule for the next month.

We only had four weeks before filming Series Seven, so I didn't have much time to make money during the break. I cracked on with the personal appearances, but I did have some limited time off too.

I spent a day at Chester Rocks, the music festival, and mingled with the VIPs in the celeb tent. The Wanted were playing live, so I made my way backstage to watch them perform. When they finished, I saw Tom Parker milling around the crowd and was determined to get a picture with him – but he came over before I had a chance to make an approach.

'I so want to be in *Geordie Shore*,' he said, shaking my hand enthusiastically.

GAZ (AND MY PARSNIP)

'I want to be in The Wanted,' I laughed, trying to conceal my surprise. Tom Parker was a megastar, much more famous than I am. What on earth was he doing talking to me?

We sat down and had a chat, swapping numbers before I left. I didn't think anything would come of it, but a few days later I was leaving a club after a PA when he walked in and grabbed me. 'You're not going anywhere,' he said, dragging me back inside.

So we had a few drinks and eventually got on the karaoke machine together. I was actually singing with Tom from The Wanted! I couldn't believe it. Fame definitely had its perks.

Wayne Rooney was tweeting about the show, Piers Morgan was tweeting me personally asking for favours – this kind of fame was beginning to feel almost normal now, and that was bad, because I wanted the novelty of it to last. I never wanted to be so world-weary as to take it all for granted.

Four weeks wasn't really enough time to rest before filming again, but by now they were paying me a lot of money to appear in the show, so I wasn't going to complain.

But it meant that I'd hardly had time to unpack from my time in Oz before I was packing again for Series Seven.

As I made my way back to the *Geordie Shore* house, I wondered what the next month would have in store for us all. Last season we'd lost Dan and Ricci and they were never replaced. I was expecting a new housemate, and couldn't wait to meet them.

I was in such high spirits.

However I had no idea just how bizarre and explosive things were going to be this time.

It was great to be back in the Newcastle house. Everyone looked like they'd had a decent night's sleep or two, had revamped their wardrobe and they were in a good mood. And we did indeed have a new housemate – Marnie Simpson, who was Sophie's cousin.

She was a cutie, a bit mad and a massive flirt. Scott loved her instantly, as did the rest of the lads. But the girls? They felt threatened, of course.

It was obvious things were going to be rocky between Marnie and the other girls from the very beginning, which put Sophie in a difficult position. She would have to stick up for her, which could cause arguments between her and the others.

Marnie was a little live wire, and I actually knew her personally already. She had dated one of my friends, which immediately put her in the no-shag area. Besides, the stick I'd get from the girls for pulling her just wouldn't be worth it. I very quickly decided the parsnip was going to steer very clear of her.

Scott, however, didn't have any loyalties to anyone, and looked very interested in our new housemate. Holly was going to be very upset if they got together. Would we ever have a totally peaceful season?

At the end of the first night, Holly decided to pre-empt things by telling Marnie that she would be upset if she and Scott became an item. The ball was in Marnie's court now. She knew that if she shagged Scott there would be grave repercussions. She had to decide: friendship with the girls or a tumble between the sheets with Scott.

She chose wrong.

On the very first night, Scott sneaked into her room and snogged her on the bed. They were trying to be discreet, but it was obvious what they were up to. Vicky went and broke it up, and then Holly got very upset at Scott's behaviour. I went to bed to remove myself from the situation.

But I wasn't even safe there, because a bit later Charlotte came into my room completely out of the blue and started to undress. She was absolutely mortal, and I knew things could go horribly wrong if I didn't take charge of the situation. So I picked her up and put her to bed, ignoring her when she kindly said I could 'have some' if I wanted.

I was proud of my restraint.

What a first night.

Next day we all sat down and wrote a bucket list of things we had always wanted to do. It was a kind of bonding exercise and we thought that maybe over the next few weeks we could do some of the things we listed. The idea was that it might shake things up a bit. If we were concentrating on something other than shagging and partying, maybe we'd all get on with each other a lot better.

Holly said she wanted to ride a motorbike. James said he wanted to learn how to fly a plane. Scott wanted to be fired out of a cannon, jump off a building wearing a wingsuit, and search for the Loch Ness monster in Scotland. Vicky wanted to learn to drive and take a muscle car along Route 66. Sophie wanted to party in the Playboy Mansion. Charlotte said she wanted to keep chickens.

Excited at the prospect, she immediately phoned up a chicken farm and organised a trip to buy some. In the end the aspiring poultry farmers returned with two and named them Rachel and Elizabeth. I was fine with it. We already had a house full of animals – a couple of extra chickens couldn't make anything worse.

We tried to play a trick on Charlotte by putting some eggs

from the fridge into the chickens' enclosure. She was so excited when she first saw them and waved them proudly around, praising the two hens for their egg-laying abilities. But eventually her and Vicky saw the date stamp on the eggs and realised what we'd done. It was very funny.

The Scott and Marnie situation got tenser and tenser. They were kissing secretly in the back alleyways of clubs, sleeping in bed together – in fact doing just about everything short of shagging.

And because she wouldn't shag him, Scott decided to go on the pull with me. Things were going well until, hilariously, Marnie decided to cockblock him.

When I woke up the next morning and saw that Scott's bed was empty, it was pretty obvious that he'd crept into Marnie's room during the night. But when we asked him to tell us what had happened he said that they hadn't shagged.

She was totally playing him. It was too funny.

The girls weren't laughing though. Marnie denied that anything had happened when they questioned her on the matter, but they weren't stupid. She was playing a dangerous game and, sure enough, the house erupted in a matter of days.

After a night out on the pull, Scott went into the shag pad with a bird, and I went to my room with a lass whom I'd brought back.

Marnie went storming into the shag pad and interrupted Scott's sex fest. He had a hard-on and he was angry that he couldn't finish his business, so he started going mad with frustration, before finally leaving the house to calm down.

Just a normal night in the *Geordie Shore* house, then.

Then things went weirdly downhill.

Vicky and Holly were arrested on suspicion of assault and

filming was dramatically halted as they were taken away for questioning. It was mad and we had no idea what was going on because we hadn't seen anything occur.

The girls were released on bail and no one knew what was going to happen next. Eventually Holly came back to the house, because she'd been released with no charge. But Vicky didn't return and we had no idea if she ever would.

Then, on Holly's birthday, we all woke up to find that Sophie was gone from the house too. And she definitely wasn't coming back.

We heard that she'd allegedly been caught on camera making some kind of racist comment on a night out and had been removed from the house because of it. What was happening to us all? Was any of it true?

It felt weird celebrating Holly's birthday when we were so confused as to what was going on.

We all tried to have fun but we were worried about our mates and didn't have any real information about what had happened.

The days passed in a bit of a blur. We had a job to do and somehow we had to do it despite how we felt about the situation.

We were being paid to entertain people with our antics, and although all we wanted to do was mope around, it was necessary to be professional, put our feelings to one side and continue filming the show.

Pushing it all out of our minds, we focused on other, less important things – like Holly's sudden penis fear, Marnie's play for Scott, and going out and getting smashed.

Holly had apparently developed a strange and funny aversion to cocks during our time in Australia – probably because she wasn't getting any action – and we all thought it was hilarious. She said it was a 'medical condition', but I reckoned it was just a way of getting some poor lad to offer her his help to get over it: by shagging her.

As I said before, Marnie was a flirty little thing and I enjoyed cheekily messing about with her, but there was nothing else to it. She and Scott were on and off, and there was no way I'd get involved with her anyway.

One night, I worked on a bar crawl with her and we had a wicked time together. But the girls had some kind of suspicion that we were going to get it on, so they decided to spy on us.

While they secretly watched from afar, we played the ice-cube game to get the bar crawl really banging. I knew that if anyone saw us passing the ice cube between our mouths they'd get the wrong idea. But as far as I was concerned there was nothing going on between us at all – so when she said she was dying to give us a kiss I was so shocked I had to ask her to repeat herself.

Was she mad?

Scott would kill me!

I stuck to my guns, even when she sat on my face during a sex position demonstration a little later on. It was hard refusing her – she was hot and she was laying it on thick. But I couldn't do it: it just wouldn't be worth it.

Instead, we finished work and went to rejoin the others at a club. Everyone was acting strangely, even Scott, who was bizarrely eyeing me with suspicion. I couldn't work out what was wrong with him.

Eventually Charlotte came over and said cryptically: 'Don't think I don't know what went on tonight.'

I didn't know what she was talking about. But it soon

became apparent that she thought I was doing something with Marnie behind Scott's back. I tried to tell her she was way off, but everyone could see us arguing and they took it as confirmation that something had happened while I'd been working with Marnie. I'd been a good mate and turned her away, even though she'd practically jumped me. Why was I getting shit for it?

I had to nip it in the bud and called Scott over to confront him. He was my mate – why was he pieing me without even asking me straight out whether anything had happened?

'If you have a problem with me in the future, face it then. Until then, wait,' I told him. I was angry with them all for jumping to such a rash conclusion. This time, I knew with absolute certainty I had done nothing wrong at all.

Marnie stepped in and tried to do damage control but she just made things worse. Suddenly everyone was screaming at everyone else and no one knew what was going on. Holly and Marnie starting yelling at each other – and a furious ball of fake hair and nails appeared on the dance floor. The bouncers tore them apart, while James held Charlotte back to stop her wading in too. She wanted to vent her anger at Marnie as well, and she unceremoniously screamed that she hated her.

Marnie stormed off, announcing that she was never coming back. Holly and Charlotte were in tears, blaming Marnie for ruining everything in the house.

'Since she arrived it's been hell,' they wept.

I had no time for it. I went in one direction, Scott went in another – nothing had happened, and yet our world was imploding. I returned to the house but when I got there, Scott and Marnie were still absent.

Our house was down from nine to four in a matter of weeks

and we were miserable as sin. The next day, we all sat around with faces likes smacked arses.

Thank God then, for Jay.

When he walked through the door to surprise us we all instantly felt better. Daddy was back and we knew if anyone could sort us out it was him. He sat us down and told us to tell him in detail what had been going on. It felt so good to talk it through.

I wanted Scott to come back so that I could explain that nothing had happened with Marnie. He was my mate and I was loyal to him. I didn't want to lose his friendship over absolutely nothing at all.

Jay called him and convinced him to come back in time for a trip to Scotland that we'd been planning. He had to be there – we were only going so that we could search for the Loch Ness monster and tick something off his bucket list.

Charlotte, Jay and Holly picked him up on the way and listened to why he was still upset with me. He genuinely thought I'd been disloyal and got it on with Marnie, which couldn't be further from the truth.

I travelled with James and as soon as I saw Scott in Scotland, eating haggis with the girls, I knew I had a chance to sort things out, and I did – convincing him that I'd stayed loyal to him all along.

We went off in search of the famous Loch Ness monster, racing around the loch in a high-speed rib. It was so much fun, but we had no chance of finding the creature in the boat, so we jumped in to have a swim around. Alas, the beast was hiding. We didn't catch a peep of him all day. We checked into a hotel in Glasgow and with Marnie not there, I knew we'd have a good time that night.

The atmosphere in the club was amazing. With Jay there our little family, much depleted as it was, had the best time ever.

I hoped Marnie wouldn't be back, because if she did our fragile peace was sure to be blown apart again. She was a nice lass, but she was a bit naïve and was bound to cause trouble, even if she didn't mean to.

But eventually she did return. Me and James were the only ones there at the time – we were in the garden when she arrived and it was probably best that it was just us. At least we could give her a friendly welcome back before everyone else turned up.

Scott came home a bit later and was obviously buzzing to see Marnie. He was actually really keen on her and I began to think that maybe she had only flirted with me to make him jealous... She obviously liked him.

Whatever the reason, the situation needed to be sorted. And for that to happen, the girls needed to accept Marnie back into the fold. And that wouldn't happen without one hell of a ding-dong.

Before they'd even seen her, Charlotte and Holly started making their protest at her return very obvious. I was barbequing our tea outside, and they were behaving like they'd just been released from the zoo.

Marnie stayed upstairs, alone, and it must have been horrible for her. She could hear Charlotte ranting and raving about how she was a slag and if she had any sense she should leave. Eventually she couldn't take it any more and came down and started defending herself.

The lads stayed outside while the girls yelled at each other indoors. All we could hear was screeching and wailing and it started to give me a headache. I was grateful I had the sausages to focus on. They were going to be the best burnt sausages ever, with all the detailed attention I was paying them.

We didn't know what to do. If we spoke to Marnie we'd get it in the neck from the girls. But the unfortunate girl was all alone and sad and it didn't seem very fair at all.

That night we went out while she stayed at home by herself. Surprisingly, the girls were keen for me and Scott to chat up some girls, which was a turn-up for the books. Normally they hated it when we went off on a pulling spree.

We knew they were only encouraging us in order to piss Marnie off, and it felt a bit sly and manipulative. Neither of us brought girls back that night, because we didn't think it was right to do so.

Instead, Charlotte was ultra friendly to me and we ended up in the shag pad, laughing and joking with each other like old times.

Nothing happened, but it was nice to feel that we might possibly be able to get back to how we were before all our dramas started.

Eventually Marnie broke down and approached the girls, sobbing. Her action knocked away a barrier of some kind, and we watched in amazement as the women actually made up. World War Number 105 in the *Geordie Shore* house was over at last.

Soon after, I met Charlotte's boyfriend, Mitch, and at first we got on like a house on fire. He was such a sound lad and I just wanted him to like me so that Charlotte and I could be mates.

But then I saw him reduce Charlotte to tears after getting

himself mortal drunk and I didn't know what to think. I couldn't believe how much of a prick he had suddenly become.

I didn't want anyone treating her like that, but what could I do? It was her choice. She had been talking about him for so long and he'd really embarrassed her. I felt sorry for Charlotte.

Despite all the usual drama, the added drama and the downright *unbelievable* extra drama, we had a wicked time filming Series Seven. MTV pulled out all the stops, maybe to compensate for losing Vicky and Sophie, and we did some crazy things. We went waterfall jumping, we flew a four-seater plane over Newcastle, we went to London, we did some rap jumping down the side of a building – it was high-octane fun and we loved it.

But it had to end, like it always does, and soon enough we were all saying goodbye again. Until the next time...

PARSNIP POINTERS

NO. 20: PLAYING THE NUMBERS GAME

When you're out on the pull, the best way to guarantee your success is to rely on the law of averages. Basically, this means that the more girls you approach the more chance you have of finding a girl who will go home with you. It's simple but beautiful.

You have to be ruthless when you're using this tactic. If you're not getting anywhere with one lass, you have to quickly move on.

Be nice about it – you never know when you might run into her again in a more giving mood – but don't waste your precious time on a girl who isn't up for it if you're only out for a one-night stand.

This is a good way to practise your other techniques and build up your pulling confidence too, so even if you're approaching loads of girls unsuccessfully every night it's by no means a wasted effort.

If you're not getting anywhere you could even try some new techniques that you're unsure of, to see if they work. It's much easier to feel confident and give something a go if you're not relying on things to work out with only one girl every night.

CHAPTER 21

SO WHAT'S NEXT?

And so here I am. A cheeky lad from Newcastle who somehow ended up on TV. A lad who had previously lurched from career to career, never really settling or being satisfied with anything. A lad whose main strengths were partying and pulling women, and who now has found a way to make money out of those exact same skills.

People say you're lucky if you find a job you love. I'm very lucky. Right now, I couldn't imagine doing anything else... I never thought I'd own a Ferrari, or my own business, or have anything like the kind of life I'm living right now.

Alongside my TV exploits I've signed a deal with condom manufacturers Skins to bring out my own range of parsnip protectors and I've joined forces with a nutritional supplement maker to create VIDAR Nutrition, a series of products that help promote a healthy way to get a ripped body like mine.

I helped to develop and design three bespoke supplements – the VIDAR Thermo-Shock, VIDAR Pre-Shock and VIDAR

After-Shock products, which consist of a fat burner, a collagen and a detox supplement and which are designed for both men and women.

They're for people like me who want to 'play hard, train hard and stay hard' and I'm very pleased with them.

I'm also about to open my very own beach club in Zante, Greece, called Pure. My thinking was that I love clubs so much, why shouldn't I open one myself? I've certainly been in enough of them to know what works and what doesn't. It's set to open in summer 2014 and it's going to be the coolest place on the island, I guarantee it. I can't wait to party there and I hope you lot will join me, too!

Plus I might open a second shop seeing as the first one is doing so well, and who knows how many more series of *Geordie Shore* we'll make?

The show's ratings have consistently climbed and climbed – we now regularly have over a million people tuning in to watch us drink, shag and wee ourselves. It's TV gold.

It has even benefited our beloved city, which has seen a huge boost in tourism since the show began. Up to four times as many people now visit Newcastle and sample its nightlife, visiting the clubs we are so often seen partying in. I'm proud to have helped make that happen.

The show will continue as long as people keep watching it. And as long as it continues, I'll want to be a part of it because it really is the perfect job for me.

But it's sometimes hard seeing yourself on TV, especially when you know there is more to you than people think. No one can ever know anyone just from seeing them on a TV show. I decided to write this book to give everyone an insight into who I really am.

SO WHAT'S NEXT?

Charlotte has often called me some very bad names – as have the rest of the cast. But they're my family and family are allowed to get mad at you every now and again. Or very often, as it sometimes must seem to our viewers...

I've been called a slag, a snake, sneaky, untrustworthy... the list goes on. But I'm a good lad really, I promise. And I still don't think I've ever really done anything wrong on the show.

When I'm loved-up, I'm a good boyfriend, devoted to my girl. But right now I'm single, and until I find that special person I'm going to have fun, and that means I can sleep with as many girls as I like. There's no law against it. I always try to treat girls with respect and people definitely know what they're getting into when they kiss me in a club or bar.

I'm not trying to be something I'm not on the show. What you see is what you get. But you only see one part of my personality on *Geordie Shore*. You're not going to see that other side of me – the caring boyfriend side, the responsible side – because on the show I'm single and free and out to have a good time.

People have seen me hurting Charlotte, but I never wanted to. We care about each other. It's just we'd never work as boyfriend and girlfriend. Not right now, anyway.

And seeing Ricci and Vicky, and other couples on the show, literally in meltdown mode, has proved to me that you can't be in a relationship while doing *Geordie Shore*. It's pretty much impossible, or at the very least it makes things very difficult.

I'm young, I'm free, and until that changes I'll keep living this lifestyle. It won't last forever – I don't want it to last forever. But for now, I'm having the time of my life. I'd love to live in Australia some day, but I've got a crazy year planned ahead of me and who knows how long all this exciting madness will last for.

When it all ends, like everything does, I'll hopefully have made enough money to give my future wife and kids a comfortable lifestyle. One I can be proud of.

And if my *Geordie Shore* legacy is to teach other lads how to be prolific pulling machines, then that's all good.

Someone's got to take over the mantle when I retire.

Don't hold your breath, though – it'll be a long time yet.

PARSNIP POINTERS

NO. 21: ENGINEERING A THREESOME

My final tip is definitely the one I'm most proud of… After the threesome in Cancun was aired, a lot of people asked me how I managed it. At first I didn't really know what to say, and it has taken me a long time to really come up with the right answer.

A threesome is the holy grail of shagging – not only have you managed to pull, but you've pulled two birds and managed to make them both want you enough to share you. You're an instant legend.

A lot of people think it's luck, or just the fact that those particular girls were a bit bisexual, but it's more than that – it's down to you to make it happen.

I've actually had quite a few threesomes, foursomes and even a fivesome once. A lot of them have been with girls who have never done it before, and who didn't even know the other girls involved. It's all about timing, and holding back.

So, you're in a club and you have two girls who are

obviously interested. Pay attention to both of them. Don't kiss either of them – if they see you kissing the other one they'll think you're not bothered about them.

Instead, just chat and be friendly to them both. Flirt with them equally, buy them a few drinks and make them both feel comfortable with you.

Start dropping into the conversation how you'd love both of them to come back to yours for a few drinks, so that at the end of the night they're not ready to go home because they want to continue the party.

Once you've got them back, start to flirt a little more with them both. Make them laugh, make them feel chilled and at ease. Once things start to wind down, suggest that you all go and share the bed to go to sleep. Don't mention a threesome. They'll be a little confused – you've not tried to kiss them, you're being gentlemanly and nice. Bide your time. It'll all be for the best.

In bed, make sure you're in the middle, and cuddle them both close to you. Everyone's happy, everyone's comfortable, everyone's starting to feel a little horny...

This is where you start working your magic: if they're friends, ask them if they have ever kissed each other before. If they're strangers, ask if they've ever kissed a girl before.

If the answer to either of these questions is yes, dare them to do it. Let them get on with it for a while, and then start to get involved. Don't wait too long – you don't want to get jealous of your bedfellows before you start shagging.

After that, things will progress nicely until you have so many holes to fill you won't know where to begin. Score.

If they've not kissed a girl or each other before, start by gently kissing one girl, before turning to kiss the other.

Don't spend too long on one girl – you don't want the second girl to start feeling awkward, while you're getting hot and heavy with the first.

If one girl jumps out of bed in a huff, it's unlikely the other will stay behind and fuck you, knowing her mate is raging in the next room.

Keep kissing them both, until they're so hot and bothered their hands start to wander, in search of more action. You'll be able to tell pretty quickly if they're going to be up for exploring each other, or if they both just want you.

If you feel a double parsnip grab – both girls clutching your cock – it's going to be all down to you. Remember to share the love equally between the two girls.

If you're grabbing a boob and you feel another hand trying to cop a feel too, then they'll be fine playing with each other while you fuck each of them in turn. You can take your time ramming them. This is the ideal scenario.

Either way, once they're both in bed and kissing you, you're pretty much guaranteed some double action.

Just make sure you don't leave either of them out for too long. Keep swapping round so that they each get what they want. You've got to be courteous, after all.